Higher Education Reconceived

Higher Education Reconceived

A GEOGRAPHY OF CHANGE

Sherrie Reynolds and Toni Craven

TCU Press
Fort Worth, Texas

Library of Congress Cataloging-in-Publication Data

Reynolds, Sherrie, 1952-
  Higher education reconceived : a geography of change / by Sherrie Reynolds and Toni Craven.
      p. cm.
  Includes bibliographical references and index.
  ISBN 978-0-87565-391-4 (alk. paper)
  1. Education, Higher--Aims and objectives--United States. 2. Education, Higher--Philosophy--United States. 3. Educational change--United States. I. Craven, Toni. II. Title.
  LA227.4.R48 2009
  378.73--dc22
                                    2008034702

TCU Press
P. O. Box 298300
Fort Worth, Texas 76129
817.257.7822
http://www.prs.tcu.edu

To order books: 800.826.8911

Cover image: Courtesy of Jeff Saward, photographer.

Designed by fusion29

We dedicate this work to

Diane Murray

and

Kathryn Craven,

*with thanks for their support
in its making and in life.*

Contents

INTRODUCTION

Labyrinths

This best known of all floor labyrinths fills the nave of Chartres Cathedral in France. It dates to the thirteenth century and measures 42.3 feet in diameter. Though little documentation remains about its purpose, it is known that labyrinths in French cathedrals were the scenes of Easter dances carried out by the clergy. **Courtesy Jeff Saward, photographer.**

Labyrinths are over 4,000 years old. The original ones appeared in the middle of the third century B.C. in Egypt. The labyrinth was an experiential teaching about the journey of life. . . . The complex twisting patterns of a labyrinth have many loops. They take one back and forth, almost retracing the same path. Nearly all labyrinths were intended to be maze-maps reflecting each person's journey to God.

From a flyer prepared by the Dominicans

The labyrinth on the cover is patterned after that at Chartres, France, which was laid into the floor of the central body of the cathedral in front of the main altar sometime between 1194 and 1220.[1] In 1995, an outdoor terrazzo replica of this most famous labyrinth was constructed at Grace Cathedral in San Francisco. As Canon for Special Ministries, Lauren Artress first reintroduced this meditative tool in 1991 as a floor canvas in Grace's nave. Her aim as a priest and psychotherapist was to find a spiritual tool that could help people change by bringing together the world of the rational and intuitive, the finite and the infinite.[2] Literally thousands worldwide are now part of Grace's Labyrinth Network.[3] This practice has spilled over into numerous local settings, and many now know for themselves what it is to walk a labyrinth.

Labyrinths, ancient and modern, are sacred paths that take many shapes and forms. Some are designed for walking, while others suggest visual journeys. Made of tiles, stones, grass, hedges, canvas, or other elements, they are found in churches, gardens, and ordinary public or private spaces. Graphic representations of labyrinths also appear on coins and pottery, or as architectural ornamentation.

A labyrinth journey begins with entrance through a gateway at its perimeter onto a winding course that proceeds unimpeded, though not always directly, toward a center. The decision to begin and travel inward, the reaching of the center, and the journey outward traditionally hold interconnections and recognitions for the seeker of births and deaths in the internal life. Connections in the life of the seeker can emerge from its process of taking an imaginative voyage with patterned, relational features many find sacred.

We think of the labyrinth as an open figure that functions as an emblem for our journey into modern and post-modern features of higher education. Like a labyrinth, the winding pathway of meaningful teaching/learning has many loops, taking one back and forth, sometimes closer and other times further from the heart of the matter. We believe that teachers and learners are part of an important relational process governed more by values than by rules.

The various labyrinths that begin each chapter of this book are meant to give a face to some aspect of change and its geography. Though all these representations are only two dimensional and unicursal, we hope that you will imagine them as multi-dimensional and porous, understanding that this is a journey in which there are many different ways to get to the heart of the matter. This journey is never without backtracking, leaving the path, and even going where there is no path.

Meeting the Authors

Sherrie Reynolds

I am sitting in my office at the university listening to a compact disc of the Benedictine monks of Santo Domingo de Silos and reading a book about learning. This convergence of the spiritual and cognitive is a metaphor for my life, and it says a great deal about why I wanted to write this book with Toni Craven. I am a university professor with a master's in Counseling and a Ph.D. in Psychology. My research is in post-modern thought. My counseling practice was in Roman Catholic communities. It seems fitting to me that a learning theorist with an interest in religion and spirituality and a Hebrew Bible scholar with an interest in education would team up to write about teaching and learning with adults in communities situated in seminaries, divinity schools, and universities.

One of the reasons this book is important to me is that I have a special relationship with learning, dating back to my very young years. I was a non-traditional college student, to say the least. I was in college on a dare because a teacher who had befriended me told me that no one thought I could make it. I was going to prove I could do it. Of course, I had no idea what college was about or if I could really do it, but there I was. It was a major turning point in my life. I remember discovering that I could learn and think, that I could take the pictures in my mind, put words around them, put them next to one another, and see something new. It was exhilarating. I fell in love with learning.

With that beginning, you can imagine that I also became interested in how people think and learn. When I started Ph.D. work, I naturally migrated to psychology hoping that I would learn more about why people are the way they are and how thinking develops or fails to do so. It is an odyssey that still occupies me and one I still find fascinating.

As a new Ph.D. student, I only knew that psychological facts and theories were presented with the authority of experiment as the current state of truth. But the descriptions of learning we studied, the ideas and "facts" that I encountered did not seem to bear much resemblance to the lived experience of learning. Learning, and in fact all human behavior, seemed messy, complex, difficult to untangle. The ideas I was learning seemed overly simplified and narrow. The categories seemed artificial and removed from everyday life. I did not know that this was the beginning of my struggle with the ideas underlying modern thought. One of my professors, however, asked me why he was fated with a doctoral student who wanted to "undermine the entire foundation of psychology."[4]

The quest to find better ways to teach erupted for me one day when I was in the middle of a class period. I was teaching in a school of education, but I was teaching as if I was still working with psychology majors. I was lecturing about fascinating theories but recognized, mid-lecture, that I was bored. I looked out at the tops of the students' heads and realized that I seldom saw their faces. They had their heads bowed, dutifully writing down what I was saying. Even if I gave them printed notes ahead of time, they wrote. I stopped in the middle of that lecture, asked them to put their pens aside, and began to talk with them. It was terrifying. I struggled to see how my understanding of learning influenced my teaching. It didn't. They were so separated that teaching was more like performance than it was like creating conditions for learning.

Later, I interviewed teachers who had taken educational psychology in school. I asked them, "What do you remember from your educational psychology class?" These teachers of all ages said, "Nothing." I decided that I wanted to change that. I began by thinking about what psychology has to offer teachers. That was not an easy question to answer. I thought about what I know about learning and how that might inform my teaching. I interviewed excellent professors and students. Over time, gradually, I became a very good teacher, and I haven't been bored in years.

My research interests entwine the study of the "New Sciences" (sometimes known as chaos and complexity theories) and cognition. I have had a lifelong affinity for the sciences and, similarly, an enduring curiosity about how humans construct knowledge. As I have come to see the foundational assumptions on which cognitive science, and indeed, all modern thinking rest, I began to engage in a difficult process of de-constructing my own assumptions about teaching and learning. Using the lenses of the new sciences, I have constructed a new way of thinking about these processes. This endeavor was messy, surprising, sometimes meandering, painful, joyful, blessed, and cursed. It was, in other words, a very human process.

My primary interest today is in the reform of colleges and universities. I still believe universities can be one of the great contributors to democracy, freedom, and the American dream. A nun who taught first year students at a university once said, "Every year they arrive waving their new minds like so many shiny new tennis rackets." I am interested in the care of these shiny new minds. Being a university professor is a sacred trust, and I am committed to upholding that trust.

Most of us have been thrust out of doctoral programs into colleges, divinity schools, or universities with little or no preparation for the teaching side of the professoriate. In the chapters that follow, Toni and I will introduce you to the ideas that have helped us reconceive learning and transform our teaching. We salute you as teachers and hope that our scholarship and life experience are useful to you.

Toni Craven

One of the lenses through which I make sense of the world is my discipline, known variously as Old Testament or Hebrew Bible.[5] I deeply value the opportunity to teach others about this literature. I sense the holiness of teaching and learning and count it a privilege to be part of a process that permits entry into the vast religious and secular findings of my academic area. On good days, I sense the sacramental nature of what I do as potentially life changing for the students, as it has been for me, and for others whom our lives may touch. At such times, it is easy to believe that teaching matters and that the work of ministry and theological education makes a real difference in our world.

There are other times, however, when trivialities shut out any larger vision and I do not perceive the ground on which I stand as holy (see Exod. 3:5). Institutional obligations feel more like forced bondage than service. I feel pulled and pushed in too many directions by what seems an inevitable collision of demands and lack of time. When duty—not fidelity—drives my actions, I feel far from anything that energizes my work or gives my teaching direction. I feel fully faithful to nothing—not to my students, not to my discipline, institution, or myself. There is little access to anything that seems transformative about teaching and learning in such barren times.

I have learned across the years that such seemingly unproductive periods often mask emerging desire for something better. Such times can serve to open my eyes to change that is already underway, or change that I am resisting, or even change that I am wishing for but am afraid will not happen for one reason or another. Experience has taught me the value in persisting through the uncertainty of such times, in waiting faithfully for that which is coming to birth, however slowly.[6]

Substantive change often includes endings that may seem like deaths of sorts, some welcomed and others resisted. Nevertheless, I believe that the miracle of new life, new growth, and new vision born of such times can reshape us, often helping us to find new heart and new bearings for ourselves as scholars, for our institutions, and for our students. Working with Sherrie has been revitalizing for me. It is the fruit of our time together and with others who shared their ideas about teaching and learning with us that we wish to pass on to you in this book.

The problem of naming my discipline holds what I consider an important key to finding new direction. "Old Testament" is ambiguous and imprecise, variously including thirty-nine books for Protestants, forty-six books for Roman Catholics, and fifty-one or more for Orthodox Christians. Worse, "Old Testament" can be a stake to Christian superiority: the "Old" eclipsed by the "New," more fully revelatory, word of God.[7] And though Hebrew is the original language of most of the literature, "Hebrew Bible" is inexact because portions of certain books—small pieces of texts, to be sure—are in Aramaic (Dan 2:4-7:28; Ezra 4:8-68 and 7:12-26; Jer 10:11; and two words in Gen 31:47). *Tanakh* (or *Tenakh*)—an acronym formed from the initial Hebrew letters of *torah* (law), *nebiim* (prophets), and *ketubim* (writings)— and *Mikra* belong to the Jewish community and are names that are strange and unfamiliar to most Christians.[8]

Further complicating this problem is what to call the eighteen books or additions to books that fill out the larger Old Testament canons of Roman Catholic, Greek Orthodox, and Russian Orthodox Christians. But from this additional difficulty came what I regard as a special blessing from the 1989 New Revised Standard Version translation committee. The NRSV uses a "slashed" alternative name: "Apocryphal/Deuterocanonical Books." This small but mighty forward slash cut through generations of division among various religious communities. Protestants can find their "Apocrypha," while Catholics and Orthodox Christians can find their various Deuterocanonical (second canon) books that fill out the differing versions of the Old Testament. I treasure this forward slash or diagonal mark (technically a virgule or solidus) for giving us the most widely shared Bible (or more precisely, Bibles)[9] in modern history. This sign, usually a separator of alternatives such as "and/or," brings together many traditions in the NRSV. By analogy, I suspect higher education needs some similar forward way of thinking that will bring together multiple perspectives, various practices of learning/teaching, and make room for traditions of excellence and diversity of all sorts. For a number of reasons that we will share in this book, I no longer think of teaching as separate from learning. I have reaffirmed my belief that teaching/learning is a lifelong reality. I want students to be doing both simultaneously. And I want to be doing both always.

As a consequence of bringing together teaching/learning, I no longer think that good teaching is objective or verified by the production of students who can ingest and repeat huge bodies of facts. I want to be part of a community of teaching/learning that fosters rich relationships of many sorts. I want to be part of a shared process of fostering environments in which we can all come to understand and appreciate more fully our connections to our pasts even as we find courage to take this day's steps toward a future whose features are as yet unclear. I yearn to be more conscious of how ordinary everyday experience is a locus of what I think of as the extraordinary reality of God's holy presence and spirit.

Across my twenty plus years of graduate theological teaching, without realizing it, I constructed a set of ideas about the role and authority of the teacher and the receptivity of learners that privileged my own agency. I thought it was my job to construct classes and to take responsibility for what the students learned. Work with Sherrie, students, and other colleagues realigned some of my views, deconstructed others, and helped me to make some significant changes.

For a long time I have believed that a community of learning needs to play an ongoing role in the construction of ideas about teaching and learning. But I have not always understood the presuppositions I brought to the construction of such a community and the distribution of power within it. While I have said for years that I want us all to find our voices—students, teachers, others, and text(s)—it is only recently that I have begun to understand how this might be accomplished more equitably. I hope you will join us in reconceiving higher education as we bring you our stories and experiences with teaching and learning. As a feminist literary-rhetorical critic, I believe that our remembered narratives tell who we are and how we make meaning.[10] We create the present and a "usable past" through the understandings we construct individually and communally.[11] In my opinion, we cannot afford to forget that such narratives also hold us accountable.

Theological education, indeed higher education in general, is crossing multiple thresholds of change. What we value and devalue, hold true or question is undergoing major reorganization. While not always easy or pain-free, I believe that the changes ahead of us hold wonderful and significant gifts for each of us. They are the signs and wonders for our generation and even the next.

Mapping the Journey

This book does not provide answers, blueprints, or procedures for teaching/learning. Teaching is a very personal activity, and we are not trying to convince you to teach the way we do. What is important to us is that we each find the ideas and conditions that make teaching meaningful for us and that allow our students to find meaning in our classes. How we do that is as unique as our fingerprints. We hope that as you read this book you will find yourself becoming more aware of how you choose to teach and why.

We live in an age—often compared to the Enlightenment—in which deep assumptions that have formed invisible constraints are being challenged. Theological studies and cognitive science testify to changing paradigms that influence our work. We believe that learning is above all an experience of self-organization and change. Meaningful learning/teaching is an experience of deep change. Reflection on change is both a primary subject and a hoped for outcome in this book. The six chapters of *Higher Education Reconceived (HER)* address personal change, change as a process, changing ideas about consciousness, learning, curriculum, and communities of learning. Change and its geography—its physical features and the relationship between its different elements in our lives, history, and disciplines—figure throughout.

Finally, we wish to express our thanks to the Wabash Center for Teaching and Learning in Theology and Religion for its support in encouraging this work by funding three sessions on *Meaningful Teaching for Pre-tenured and Tenured Faculty at Brite Divinity School and Texas Christian University.*[12] The eleven of us who shared portions of this book in preliminary draft, meals, and conversations about teaching/learning enjoyed stimulating exchanges. One participant said nearly a year after we ended, "Our discussions soared with the eagles, not the buzzards, and I, for one, am enormously grateful."[13] Another participant noted,

> There's a tremendous amount of energy (unfortunately latent) that I see can be tapped into when I start to view the classroom as more of a meeting of the minds and an encounter rather than a packaged presentation that I give, however skillfully, to passive consumers. I've also learned, importantly, to think of my mis-steps not only as failures, but as part of the natural process of trial and error, constant correcting of the course that is yet unfolding.[14]

It is to such conversation and journey that we now invite you.

CHAPTER ONE

Personal Change

Labyrinth from Watts Chapel in Compton, England, built by Mary Watts during the nineteenth-century labyrinth revival. Four labyrinth shields held by hand-carved terra cotta angels surround the interior walls, each instructed the Way, the Truth, and the Life.
Courtesy Jeff Saward, photographer.

"Disconnecting from change does not recapture the past. It loses the future."

Kathleen Norris (*Dakota*, 64)

Sherrie Reynolds: Change

True change is a complex and difficult psychological process. This is especially true of change in teaching because teaching rests on closely held beliefs that arise from our deepest sense of our world, our selves, and others. My friend Howard Polanz calls these "baby elephant beliefs." He tells how circus elephant trainers restrain a baby elephant with a rope tied to a stake in the ground. If it tries to escape, it cannot because it is not strong enough to get free of the rope. The baby elephant adopts the belief that it cannot escape, and by the time it is grown no longer questions that belief. The adult elephant would find escape easy, but it never tries. Howard suggests that many of us have baby elephant beliefs that restrain us just as surely as the elephant's belief about the rope. It has been important for me to uncover these baby elephant beliefs, examine them, and make conscious choices about the ones worth keeping. Much of my growth as a professor has not been as much about adding new ideas as it has been about uncovering and discarding old ones that are constraining me.

Change as Process   PHASE SHIFT

Most of us think of change as linear and incremental, like adding one brick at a time. The kind of change that interests me, deep transformative change, is more adequately conceived as what chaos scientists call a "phase shift."

A phase shift is a process of change that occurs suddenly. It is a change from one kind of state to another. When I am sleeping and I awaken, I experience a phase shift. I describe it as if it is gradual, but in fact the movement from asleep to awake is a sudden change in state. Much of human experience is like that. Because it is not incremental, the process of change often feels like repeated failure rather than progress.

I conducted an informal survey for a number of years about how people stop smoking. When I asked people how they quit, they said something like "I tried and failed and tried and failed and then finally I did 'x' and it worked and I quit." Most of these people think that the *last* thing they tried is the one that works and that the other things they tried were simply failures. It interests me that something different worked for each of these people. The reason they think 'x' is the way to stop smoking is because coincidentally it was the last thing they tried before they were able to stop. The fact that one person's last thing may have been another person's first thing helps us to see that the magic is not in 'x'. What they had in common was the process of trying, failing, trying, failing, and finally succeeding.

Few of us began our careers as professors thinking about how people learn. Most of us thought, and some still think, that our job is to pass on knowledge and information that has been generated in a discipline or field of study. Many of us believed that it is the professor's job to cover certain material. We thought we had to have the answers, and that we had to be in charge or in control. At some point in our careers, we may realize that these are baby elephant ideas.

In my experience of listening to lectures, it is clear to me that ideas are not conveyed from the lecturer to us. I do not sit passively in the lecture absorbing what the lecturer says. I am thinking and going off on tangents. If I am really bored, I am only physically in the room. I may be mentally at home organizing my garage. The process of listening to a lecture is _interactive_. Both sides of the equation are important. Our ideas, beliefs, values, and understanding determine what we see, hear, and understand. In a very real sense, no two of us are actually in the same lecture. I have often thought that if we could have someone interview our students immediately after a class and have them repeat what they thought we said, we would be very surprised at the diversity of their responses. The idea that teaching is not a transfer of knowledge is difficult for many of us. This is not an easy concept to grasp. The idea that learning is directly _caused_ by teaching is one of the mainstays of our culture and our profession. We have ample evidence today to question this idea.

Change Is Messy

I once attended a concert by Roberta Flack, and at the end we gave her a standing ovation. She twirled around in ecstasy, thanked us, and said, "It only took me twenty years to become an overnight success." We tend to see the great singer, rather than the process of getting ready to become a great singer. Transformative change is really two processes: (1) preparing to change, and (2) changing. Often, like former smokers, we think of preparation for change as failure.

The process of change begins with a sense that something else is possible. There is a feeling that there is another way to be, do, or understand. At this point the feeling is so vague that we often shrug it off. We may experience brief moments of clarity while listening to someone or reading a book only to lose it again when the speaker stops or we close the book. Sometimes we doubt that we understood in the first place.

The process is frustrating and messy for a while. As we gain experience with these new ideas and begin to understand the principles that guide them, we are even more annoyed with ourselves when we have to do something in a traditional fashion. In teaching, for example, the principles are not at all clear at first, and the way to teach based on those principles is not clear all at once either.

When a principle is newly embraced, it seems to explain everything. There is a honeymoon period in early change in which this new idea seems to be the answer. But afterwards, the one who is changing begins to experience gaps, inconsistencies, and contradictions in the new idea and will likely feel off balance. There is a disquieting sense that something is not right.

Jean Piaget used the word "equilibration" to describe the process of balancing between production and conservation.[1] Equilibration is guided by a sense of internal consistency that will not let us forever hold contradictory notions. In the early stages of deep or second order change, new ideas are pasted in and the resulting gaps, contradictions, and inconsistencies are ignored. Eventually we have to reorganize and create a way of thinking that minimizes these gaps, contradictions, and inconsistencies.

Equilibration allows us to be conservative enough that there are things or ideas we can count on to give us some stability and yet open enough that we can innovate and change and grow. The balance point for each of us seems to differ based on our history and our personality. Some of us lean toward openness and seek change and novelty, while others lean toward conservation and cling to the familiar. Individually these tendencies may cause us problems, but in a group we tend to balance one another. We also tend to annoy one another.

I once asked a nun friend of mine why they used to wear habits. She said that originally the idea was to wear the garb of the common people so that they would blend in. By not changing over the years, by rigidly remaining in the same dress while those about them changed, the habit became a mark of distinction, setting nuns apart from all the rest of the people. By not changing, in this case, they changed something even more important; they changed the principle that originally guided their decision. Avoiding change is not really possible because we do not live in a static universe. Ultimately we can either embrace change or be buffeted by it. The pain associated with change is as often caused by fear and resistance as it is by the reality of our past experience of changing.

Avoiding Change

One of my colleagues avoids change by always translating the new idea in such a way that it eventually looks just like the old one. In meetings she says things like, "I think we are talking about the same thing, but using different words." On such occasions, I have been certain that we are using different words because we are talking about different things. For some of us, avoiding change is part of preparing to change. That sounds odd, but it isn't. What appears as avoidance can be simply exhausting all easier possibilities first.

There are professors who avoid change at all costs. Perhaps such avoidance is a reflection of their personal history, their immobilizing fear, or their disinterest in investing time and energy in changing. Some resist change because teaching is only a means of earning a living. The easiest thing is to keep doing what they have done in the past, because they have all their materials and lecture notes.

Another group are the change-resisters. These are the folks who are against anything new just because it is new. Usually they are not overt about this. They may act as if they are actually enthusiastic about change, but then they begin to mention little problems they see. With a new idea, this constant barrage of helpful criticisms can be devastating. Like water dripping on a rock, such criticism can erode a new idea.

Change-resisters are helpful in a strange sort of way. Frequently the most conservative professors represent a limit on one end that balances those who always want to go for the newest, freshest, most novel idea. In some ways, change-resisters force those too quick to change to think about an idea more carefully.

Those too quick to change are the bandwagon folks who jump on every new idea that comes along. Ironically, they can also avoid transformative change by appearing to adopt it wholeheartedly. I have learned over the years to be skeptical about people who seem too enthusiastically to adopt an idea that they are hearing for the first time. It is natural, with a real change, to be a bit hesitant and to drag one's feet. In fact, that is part of the way we balance psychologically so that we don't change so much that we have no sense of stability. We like to keep a rock on which to stand while we change.

Toni Craven: A Story of Change

This book emerges from over five years' work with Sherrie that began when I was directing the divinity school's brand new Ph.D. programs in biblical interpretation and pastoral theology/pastoral counseling. Because I wanted to provide opportunities for our doctoral students to think critically about teaching, as well as their disciplines, I asked Sherrie to lead two one-hour colloquium sessions for us. She set before us a captivating vision that teaching and learning is a dynamic process of change. The idea that learning is a messy interactive process—not caused by teaching—took ready root with us, and we all wanted to know more. The following year, Sherrie agreed to come for two additional one-hour sessions on teaching and learning. These were small but important steps that initiated a time of getting ready to change for the students and for me.

Out of these experiences, Sherrie and I later decided to offer a three-credit university-wide course for advanced students headed for careers in higher education, from a variety of disciplines. The second time we taught this experimental class, we began this book. I am now in the midst of an exciting and sometimes unsettling messy process of understanding and implementing changes in how I think about teaching/learning. I am deeply committed to the enduring, positive value of reconceiving teaching and learning for both beginning and seasoned teachers/learners.

In some ways, I am a novice to these complex understandings of change in teaching/learning. But in other ways, I have found that many rich ideas about change and equilibration are embedded in the literature I have taught for years, Hebrew Bible/Old Testament. My discipline provides a usable vocabulary I already know that can be used in the service of transformation and change. My discipline gives me a place of stability in the process of change, a rock on which to stand while I change. I offer the following illustration from my discipline and suggest that you think about your discipline's vocabulary and understanding of change since it is likely that you, too, have constructed your ideas about change from what you already know.

Ezekiel and Transformative Change

Ezekiel offers programmatic counsel about radical, transformative, phase-shift change, in which hearts of stone are exchanged for hearts of flesh (Ezek 36:26). This seventh-century BCE prophet to the Jewish community exiled from Jerusalem to Babylon talks at length about unsettling sudden changes of state, or phase shifts: letting go of the old to inherit the new (36:12); priests who relinquish land ownership because their inheritance is God, not land (44:28); rulers who will not dispose of the holdings of others (46:18); twelve tribes with equal shares of the land (47:13-14); and land boundaries reapportioned by God (48:29). In the disequilibrium and desolation of the exile, this prophet finds voice to say that old ways have been empty for years; it is meaningless to hope in them any longer. At the same time, he warns against false despair, holding before the exiles a vision of the restoration and new balance—equilibration—of scattered peoples and the temple.

I know of few who understand more fully than Ezekiel the transformative, reciprocal nature of change, and the fact that instruction by itself does not effect conversion. His job is to speak—or teach—whether the people heed him or not (33:30-33). The point is that doing his job brought Ezekiel life; failure to speak the words God gave him promised only death (3:20; 33:6). And this prophet knows that change is self-constructed and individual (18:1-32; 33:10-20). The time is past for repeating the proverb, "The parents have eaten sour grapes, and the children's teeth are set on edge" (18:2). "The righteousness of the righteous shall not save them when they transgress, and as for the wickedness of the wicked, it shall not make them stumble when they turn from their wickedness" (33:12).

Change and Conversion

Change is the stuff of religious as well as educational conversion. Ezekiel is not talking about linear, incremental change. One state is replaced by another for people who take responsibility for their own actions (18:1-32; 33:10-20). No virtuous acts exempt the righteous; no past sins tether the wicked. When some listeners protest that this is unfair (18:25), the prophet reports that all Israel will be judged by a God who says, "I have no pleasure in the death of anyone. Turn, then, and live" (18:32).

The prophet's final vision (40-48) also describes change as a systemic phase shift, a sudden change of state. According to the final words of the book, after twenty-five years in exile and 750 miles away from the homeland, the community is called to dwell in a place renamed *YHWH shamah,* "The LORD is There" (48:35). Those asleep to knowledge of God, misguided by false hope in easy restoration or false hopelessness that all is ended, awaken to a new reality when they take up personal responsibility and reorganize their lives accordingly. The restored community lives in a new city, the prophet says, that can be entered through twelve gates (48:30-34). These gates, not built by human hands, are there for all people.

Similarly, I believe different ways of entrance already exist in our various disciplines for reconceiving teaching/learning. Tradition undergirds our journey; poetic vision gives it heart. And the gates or ways of entry into reconceiving teaching/learning are already in place. As the fourth-century CE Cappadocian theologian Gregory of Nazianzus says:

> The scope of our art is to provide the soul with wings,
> to rescue it from the world and give it to God, and
> to watch over that which is in His image. If it abides,
> we are to take it by the hand; if it is in danger, to
> restore it; if it is ruined, to make Christ dwell in the
> heart by the Spirit. In short our task is to deify, and to
> bestow heavenly bliss upon one who belongs to the
> heavenly hosts.[2]

Relationship, interest in teaching as art, concern about life and death, realization that change is all around us, recognition that paradigms in all disciplines are shifting, such things challenge us to look more closely at what change is and what it requires. We who teach know that our students today are not exactly like we were when we were in graduate school. And as professors, many of us understand that we cannot simply imitate how our teachers taught or even what they taught.

It is increasingly clear that change is the order of the day. Ours is a culture built on fast-paced change that affects us individually and communally. In biblical studies, for instance, new methodologies and new faces at the table of critical inquiry are the norm. Diversity has become the hallmark of all theological inquiry. Gender, race, culture, sexuality, social location, and privilege are in the foreground—not the background—of methodological considerations. The challenge of change is everywhere present, pressing us to question where we are going, what we are doing, and why.

Since growth often involves uncovering and discarding constraining ideas, we need to consider the baby elephant ideas that bind us or legitimate our way of thinking. Kathleen Norris points out that Dakotans whose lives emulate the unchanging land in which they live "can lose an important aspect of their humanity. In forsaking the ability to change, they diminish their capacity for hope."[3] It is for ourselves, our students, our institutions, and for the sake of the next generation that we press on to understand change and its features, lest we learn the hard way "that disconnecting from change does not recapture the past. It loses the future."[4]

CHAPTER TWO

Emergent Change

Labyrinth floor tiles in thirteenth-century Toussaints Abbey, Chalons-sur-Marne, France, in which the classical pattern is exactly repeated four times and rotated.
Courtesy Jeff Saward, photographer.

> "'Traveling naked into the land of uncertainty' allows for another kind of learning, a learning that helps us forget what we know and discover what we need. It leads to the discovery that helps us create the future."
>
> Robert E. Quinn (*Deep Change,* 12)

First and Second Order Change

The American psychologists Paul Watzlowick, John Weakland, and Richard Fisch write about the difference between what they call first and second order change in their book *Change: Principles of Problem Formation and Problem Resolution.*[1] First order change is actually a way of trying to substitute minor change for a deeper kind of change. This is what most of us do in our initial response to a need for change. The former smokers whom I[2] interviewed talked about changing brands, cutting down, only smoking at work, only smoking at home, or reducing the number of cigarettes by one each day. These are surface or first order changes. If we are sleeping and having a nightmare, a first order change is the equivalent of changing dreams. A second order change is the equivalent of waking up.

Second order change is transformative change. As teachers/learners, we resist second order change because it requires that we rethink the nature of teaching and learning and alter most of our thoughts and actions. This kind of change does not ask us to adopt new materials or find new activities. It asks us to envision an entirely new foundation for teaching, a new relationship with students, a new way of understanding ourselves and what we do. Second order change reorganizes the very core of who we are as teachers/learners. No wonder we try to find an easier, softer way.

Change as Fractal

Our experience of change is best imaged as "fractal." Fractals are common patterns in nature but were not described until we developed what M. Jayne Fleener calls the "geometry of relationship."[3] She says that when Benoit Mandelbrot, the creator of chaos geometry (1980), was studying electronic transmissions, he noticed that

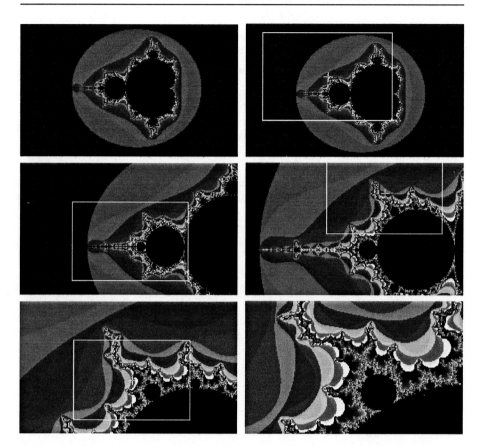

"no matter how much the transmission is amplified, there is a similarity, across scales, of noise to clear transmission and patterns seem to occur across these scales that uniquely represent the dynamics of the system."[4] He studied other problems, such as the flooding of the Nile and the fluctuation of cotton prices, and found the same dynamic characteristics. He developed fractal geometry to explore the recurring emergent patterns in the real world, not the perfect Platonic forms of Euclidean geometry.

Fractals are non-linear and are characterized by curves that are irregular all over. Interestingly, they have exactly the same degree of irregularity at all levels of scale.[5]

The images above are views of a fractal called the Mandelbrot set. Each subsequent image is the result of zooming in on part of the original figure. Notice the similarity at different levels of scale.[6]

This image of self-similarity at different levels of scale is a good description of the change in our teaching. We experienced a change at one level, which recursively affected us at other levels that we had not anticipated. This kind of reverberation or resonance through a system is one of the disconcerting things about the experience of second order change. It is not as planned and controlled as it sounds. We do some things to prepare ourselves, we are transformed, and then we begin to notice all of the ways this change shows up in our lives. It is an emergent change.

Emergent change is illustrated by what Michael Barnsley in the mid-1980s dubbed the "chaos game."[7] To play the game, as in the following illustration, you label the vertices of a triangle (any triangle works—right, equilateral, isosceles) red, blue, and green. Then label two faces of a die red, two blue, and two green. Randomly choose a point within the space of the triangle. (Close your eyes and put your pencil down, making the "seed" dot). Roll the die. In this case, let's say, the roll came up red. Choose a point halfway between the seed dot and the red dot. Make a point. If the next roll came up green, make a point halfway between the new dot and the green dot. If the next roll is blue, make a point halfway between the new dot and the blue dot. If the next roll is again blue, make a point halfway between the new dot and the blue dot.

After a thousand rolls of the die in this way suggested by Barnsley, a beautifully complex figure emerges. Intricate self-similarity at different levels of scale gives shape

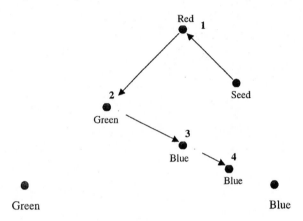

to a figure known as the Sierpinski triangle.[8] This fractal demonstrates emergent order from apparent randomness.

A triangle composed of identical red, green, and blue triangles within triangles

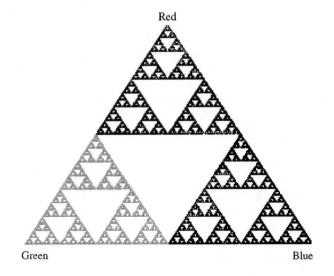

emerges one dot at a time. Such change results from unplanned, seemingly random reiterations across time. By the roll of a die, order that is non-linear in its construction clusters around an empty, open center. Boundaries and complex patterns emerge that construct a whole system of relationships in an unpredictable—yet clearly perceptible—way. Among other things, the intricate beauty of this emergent figure offers a lesson in persistence and enduring grace, especially as it relates to teaching and learning.

Teaching based on the belief that learning is emergent is very different from traditional teaching. The belief that learning emerges reverses the traditional view that teaching causes learning. It suggests, instead, that teaching is a response to learning. Teaching becomes possible when a student encounters a problem, sees a contradiction, or expresses a question.

Seeing through Old Ideas

Piaget proposed that we see through the ideas we already have and that we try to make new ideas fit with what we already know. He likened this process to the biological process of assimilation. When we eat an apple, for example, part of the apple becomes a part of us and the part we can't use is eliminated. The part that becomes us is not distinguishable; we can't point to the bit of us that is part apple. It has been assimilated; it has been mixed in with everything that already was. That is how we learn. When we are exposed to ideas, we use the parts we can and eliminate the rest. The part we cannot use does not exist for us. The part we can use becomes integrated and connected with the rest of what we know in such a way that its original form can no longer be identified separately.

When we are introduced to a new idea, we often do not hear it as something new because we try to make it fit into our old way of thinking. We grow unevenly and find ourselves trying to put new wine in old wineskins (see Mk 2:22; Mt 9:17; Lk 5:37-38). When we first changed our teaching, for example, we did not change how we taught everything. We could see how to change the way we taught certain concepts, but others eluded us. Since we had to teach these concepts, we taught them in the same way that we always had. We also changed the way we taught before we were able to change the way we graded, so there was inconsistency between assessment and teaching.

It took time for our ideas about assessment to catch up with our ideas about teaching. And we've watched some of our colleagues simply abandon assessment, believing that no assessment is consistent with their new way of teaching. Others change the way they teach but continue to give the same kind of tests (or even the same tests) that they formerly used. As these changes were occurring for us, as the deep infrastructure of our ideas about teaching was changing, we began to lose touch with the way we used to see things. We remembered, of course, that we used to teach differently, but we could not mentally recover our old frame of mind. The change was so total that we lost touch with our older way of thinking.

Second order change is a change in core beliefs and is often accompanied by enthusiasm and fervor. We all know that for a smoker, the worst person to be with is not the one who has never smoked but the one who recently quit smoking. Second order change brings with it intolerance toward those who have not yet changed and anger and frustration with those who appear unwilling to change. It feels as if suddenly we can see so clearly what needs to happen that we are impatient with those who can't yet see it. In fact, such change feels so sudden and so total that it is as if the old glasses through which we looked at the world made everything upside down and now we have new glasses that restore it aright. It can seem incomprehensible why anyone would want to continue using the old glasses.

There is, in this kind of enthusiasm, the danger of overzealous fervor. We often try to share our new insights with those around us and are disappointed at their lack of interest. Often groups begin to polarize around those who get it and those who do not. Sometimes these groups are not even civil to one another. Traditional professors may feel that they are being criticized suddenly for teaching the way they have always taught. It appears to them that the rules have changed abruptly and that previously acceptable ways of doing things are now judged outmoded. Reformed professors feel that the traditional ones are behind, blocking progress and keeping the rest from changing. We've even heard professors speak of one another as if they were enemies at war with one another. While such passion is common, it is not good, helpful, or even necessary.

The process of change is not easy, but it is potentially life giving and transformative. It calls us to rethink our foundational ideas about teaching and learning, our relationships with students, and the very core of who we are as teachers/learners. Once we experience transformative change, it reverberates throughout our assumptions and sets into motion a process of emergent change that seems to happen as if by chance. This kind of process can breathe new energy and purpose into teaching and revives careers that are stagnating.

CHAPTER THREE

Changing Ideas about Consciousness

Labyrinth from Pavia, Italy. **Courtesy Jeff Saward, photographer.**

"The kinds of nets we know how to weave determine the kinds of nets we cast. These nets, in turn, determine the kinds of fish we catch."

Elliott Eisner *(Cognition and Curriculum Reconsidered, 41)*

"Somebody once observed to the eminent philosopher Wittgenstein how stupid medieval Europeans living before the time of Copernicus must have been that they could have looked at the sky and thought that the sun was circling the earth. Surely a modicum of astronomical good sense would have told them that the reverse was true. Wittgenstein is said to have replied: 'I agree. But I wonder what it would have looked like if the sun had been circling the earth.'"

James Burke *(The Day the Universe Changed, 11)*

Bedrock Ideas

Like peeling an onion, uncovering deeply held assumptions reveals layer after layer. Assumptions held in common often appear to be reality. Common assumptions are inhaled with the air people breathe so that often they seem natural and real. These assumptions can constrain us like invisible ropes and keep us making first order substitutions instead of second order transformations.

Beliefs and assumptions formed by ideas that undergird a culture and/or time period are layered within larger narratives or interpretive frameworks. Periodically, a kind of earthquake erupts through the intellectual landscape that overturns these deeply held ideas. When bedrock assumptions topple, as in the Enlightenment, there is a phase shift in human history. We are currently living in the midst of such an era. Assumptions that have been invisible for generations are now being questioned. Bedrock ideas of the dominant culture are giving way, and a new story is emerging. Many such assumptions define and shape ideas about learning/teaching, constraining literally everything in higher education from definition of classical texts to how we construct and shape a syllabus, class discussion, assessment, and qualifying examinations.

In a marvelous satire published in 1880, *Flatland,* Edwin Abbott tells the story of A. Square, a sentient geometric shape, who journeys to the land of other two-dimensional figures. He tries to tell the points that he is a line, but no matter what he does or says, all the points can see is a point. In his frustration A. Square ventures to another land and sees a line like himself. But the line tells A. Square that he is a sphere. When a culture changes its deepest ways of understanding itself, it is as if points see others only as points, lines as lines, and spheres as spheres. A shared world is often uncomfortable or seemingly impossible when its dimensions are in transition.

The Mechanical Universe

Isaac Newton (1642-1727) synthesized the scientific knowledge of his day in a new narrative that laid the foundation for classical physics and ushered in a new era in science and invention. The metaphor for this period was the machine. Earth was a cog in a clockwork universe. It was assumed that discovery of the laws that govern the universe would lead to prediction and control. A complex phenomenon could be understood by breaking it down into parts from which one could understand the whole. Alvin Toffler describes this as "The notion that the world is a clockwork, the planets timelessly orbiting, all systems operating deterministically in equilibrium, all subject to universal laws that an outside observer could discover."[1]

During the modern period (roughly 1860 to the 1980s or, for some, to the present) experimentation became the preferred method of science. It was assumed that we had finally found a way to force nature to give up its secrets. The twentieth century has shown this to be an illusion! William Doll summarizes the certainty and control characteristic of modernism this way:

> Founded on Enlightenment thought, itself based on Cartesian certainty and Newtonian stability, and particularly on the union of this thought with industrialism, modernism developed definite social and epistemological visions. The intersection of these visions lay in the concept that improvement, progress, betterment for all would come through technology and right reason. . . . Underlying this cosmological vision was a belief or faith in certainty—that certainty was attainable through 'right reason,' and that once attained it would be lasting. Once the real structures—of mathematics and the sciences, of social and psychological situations, or reality itself—were understood, the stability of the cosmos was such that one could be certain forever.[2]

A Transition

A machine is relatively simple. It is organized hierarchically and operates linearly and predictably. Consciousness, on the other hand, is complex. It consists of many connections and interdependencies, internal and external, which make it unpredictable. Matthew Fox and Rupert Sheldrake describe such consciousness as a change from a mechanical to an organic universe:

> Instead of nature being made up of inert atoms, just inert bits of stuff enduring forever, we now have the idea that atoms are complex structures of activity. Matter is now more like a process than a thing. . . . Instead of living on an

inanimate planet, a misty ball of rock hurtling around the sun in accordance with Newton's laws of motion, we can now think of ourselves as living in Mother Earth.[3]

In the 1970s, civic and business leaders noticed a pattern of change that was occurring across several disciplines. Finding strong evidence of changes "in the shared pattern of ideas over a broad range of human inquiry, thought, and interest,"[4] they commissioned Stanford Research Institute to study these changes so that businesses could plan for the future. This consciousness, which Peter Schwartz and James Ogilvy understand as "one of the most potent forces for change in our time: a shift in humanity's image of reality and self,"[5] compares to the shift that occurred in the Enlightenment and the Copernican revolution, with the difference that this time we are aware of the shift as it is occurring.[6] Schwartz and Ogilvy suggest that "the total pattern of change is somewhat like a change in metaphor from reality as a machine toward reality as a conscious organism. . . . We are like the world we see."[7]

Schwartz and Ogilvy found a pattern within and across the various disciplines they examined. They maintain that if we overlook details, the changes in every discipline reflect a web of the following seven features:

- From simple toward complex

- From hierarchy toward heterarchy

- From mechanical toward holographic

- From determinate toward indeterminate

- From linear toward mutual causality

- From assembly toward morphogenesis

- From objective toward perspective

These features are not points on a line, distinct from one another. They are aspects of a single interconnected pattern or web. The descriptions that follow are meant to be like flashlights shining on first one aspect and then another of a unitary world.

From Simple to Complex

Simple phenomena are made up of a series of independent parts, in straightforward, linear relationships. The effects of one part on another in a simple machine can be figured out by tracing the transfer of energy from one part to another. Complicated phenomena are made up of a large number of simple relationships. These relationships can be understood through analysis and comprise much of what we discovered through traditional science.

In recent years, we have become aware of another kind of relationship, one that does not lend itself to analysis: complex relationships. Complex phenomena are interdependent and interconnected. They affect one another. Schwartz and Ogilvy liken this kind of difference to when one moves from "an isolated individual to a married couple to a family with children and finally to an extended family of cousins, aunts, and grandparents."[8] Simple relationships, in which A leads to B, are generally represented as A→B. Complex relationships are generally represented as a web in which A and B affect each other as A←→B.

In an academic field like biblical studies, exegesis (how to interpret or lead out the meaning of a text) is in a transition that illustrates the difference between complicated and complex relationships. The following two examples (the first from Hayes and Holladay; the second from Stuart) illustrate the kinds of assumptions in thinking about exegesis as a series of complicated relationships. Exegesis is described as a string of simple relationships, generally listed historically and with a sense of a right place to begin. The third example from Yee illustrates exegesis as a complex set of relationships or web that can be entered randomly at any point.

For the last twenty-five years, students have been shaped by the kinds of assumptions in the influential discussions of John H. Hayes and Carl R. Holladay, *Biblical Exegesis: A Beginner's Handbook,* the 1982 first edition of which was among the first handbooks available to succinctly introduce the subject of biblical exegesis and provide helpful bibliographies for textual criticism, historical criticism, grammatical criticism, literary criticism (as compositional and rhetorical style), form criticism, tradition criticism, and redaction criticism. Hayes and Holladay's second edition in 1987 added chapters on structuralism and canonical criticism, and their third edition in 2007 added the chapter "Exegesis with a Special Focus: Cultural, Economic, Gender, and Sexual Perspectives."[9] While their work is up-to-date and they do not suggest that the doing of an exegesis must include every type of criticism, they nonetheless encourage a synthesis of the kinds of analysis described in their book. *"Exegesis is a systematic process through which we reach an informed interpretation of a passage of Scripture"* (italics theirs).[10]

A practitioner like Douglas Stuart[11] describes exegesis as a careful, linear twelve-step process that involves (1) establishment of the text, (2) translation of the text from ancient Hebrew, Aramaic, or Greek to a modern receptor language, (3) reconstruction of the historical context of a passage, (4) understanding the literary content of a passage [itself a four-step procedure of examining literary function, placement of a text, analysis of detail, and analysis of authorship], (5) broad delineation of the general form or literary genre from one or more of the eight major biblical genres (law, historical narrative, gospel, illustrative narrative like parable and allegory, wisdom, prophecy, hymnody, and epistles), narrower identification of a literary subtype (defined by common features shared with other texts), and determination whether the passage is prose, poetry, or some mixture of the two, (6) analysis of structure (through outline, pattern analysis, descending units of size, minor patterns like the repetition of vowel sounds or verbal roots, poetic patterns such as parallelism, metric patterns, rhyme, assonance, acrostic or chiastic patterns, formulas, and other linguistic devices), (7) correct understanding of the grammar of the passage in its original language, (8) correct lexical analysis or understanding of the meaning of words and terms in a passage, (9) biblical context (how the message of a text fits into the broader body of biblical truth, or where a text is used or reused in the Bible), (10) its theology (defined by Stuart as the systematic study of revealed truth), (11) review of scholarly secondary literature on a passage, and (12) determination of the meaning or application of a passage for either its original audience or modern audience. In

Stuart's own words, "The goal of exegesis is to know neither less nor more than the information actually contained in the passage. Exegesis, in other words, places no premium on speculation or inventiveness; novelty in interpretation is not prized."[12] An accurate interpretation must pass the hermeneutical rule that "a passage cannot mean now what it could not originally have meant. That is, there is no valid modern application of the passage that was not also a potentially valid application of the passage for its original audience."[13]

Another way of thinking about biblical methods that represents complex relationships in biblical criticism is illustrated in Gale A. Yee's *Judges & Method: New Approaches in Biblical Studies*.[14] The book is dedicated to "the students we teach and who teach us."[15] Yee and eight other contributors look at the Book of Judges from the perspectives of narrative criticism, social-scientific criticism, feminist criticism, structuralist criticism, deconstructive criticism, ideological criticism, postcolonial criticism, gender criticism, and cultural criticism. In this view of interpretation, students, the authors, and the various methods inform and are informed by each other. The resulting complexity is a web of influences in which A and B have an effect on each other (A←→B). In the preface to the second edition, Yee states, "Two approaches that are quite significant for today's world, minority criticism and global criticism, are not represented in distinct essays in this volume; instead, the contributors wish through the essays that follow to underscore the importance of integrating issues of race and globalism with discussions of gender, class, colonial history, and culture in analyses of the biblical text."[16] Integration of this sort and interdependence encourage creativity and inventiveness in arranging the steps to follow in exegesis. Exegesis is a messier and less orderly process driven more by a student's perception of a problem or contradiction than by the teacher's knowledge of how to do it.

The limitations of the hierarchial paradigm of classical western scholarship that undergirds works like those by Hayes and Holladay and Stuart are increasingly evident. Different interpretive theories, use of scripture by believing and non-believing communities, and challenges posed by marginalized readers have resulted in feminist criticism, deconstruction, post-colonialism, queer theory, and interpretations from various social locations such as womanist, African American and African criticism, Asian criticism, Native American criticism, and Latina/Latino criticism. These voices have challenged ideas once widely accepted, such as correct understanding, truth, and objectivity. The interests of the academy are in transition, though we are still struggling with privileged findings.[17]

The newer methods of biblical criticism are interrelated in a way that is not linear, simple, or easily analyzed, which is likely the case for the fields of all who are reading this book. The very presence and inclusion of divergent voices testifies to the commitment of biblical studies—and by extension all contemporary fields of critical inquiry—to consciousness that the practices of a discipline are complex, interdependent and interrelated, with room for many voices and many perspectives that are not easily related.

From Hierarchy to Heterarchy

One of the consequences of the interdependence of complex phenomena is recognition of a new kind of order. In the past it was assumed that all order looked like a pyramid, a hierarchy with someone (or thing) at the top identified as being in authority and holding power (or formal precedence) over those beneath, on down a chain of command. Organizational charts of such ranked members yield clear taxonomies of relationship and responsibilities. Hierarchy is a reflection of a mechanical worldview in which anything can be seen as equal to other things on its level, as made up of parts from the level below it, or as a part in the level above it. For most of our history, this kind of vertical, top-down order is the only kind of organizational structure we have recognized commonly.

Emergent order results from the interdependence of localized elements, not from hierarchical authorization. Emergent order is, in Schwartz and Ogilvy's words, a change from "the rule by one to several rules by some."[18] To understand this distinction, consider how we sometimes use the expression "I have my ducks in a row" as a metaphor for individual mastery or control. Interestingly, though not correctly, our figure of speech suggests belief that ducks flying overhead are being led by a head duck, who is in charge of the formation. However, in a 1986 computer-generated model of coordinated animal motion using boids (generic simulated flocking creatures), Craig Reynolds demonstrated that the same results could be obtained if each boid autonomously follows simple local rules about where to fly with respect to the nearest animal. Flockmates steer to maintain three rules: separation to avoid crowding, alignment to the average heading of local flockmates, and cohesion related to the average position of local flockmates.[19] Order emerges from these local rules; it is not dictated by a supreme commander or some hierarchical authorization. It isn't even the intent of the ducks to fly in a row. There is no one duck at the head of a pyramid keeping the others in order. Rather, interactions between simple nonlinear behaviors of individuals produce emergent group behaviors. This kind of system is multi-agent and offers a metaphor for the global behavior of interacting autonomous agents. Though unpredictable, such behaviors are not random, as witness any tightly organized V-shaped row of birds overhead.

Heterarchy, not hierarchy, accounts for emergent order. Heterarchy is a form of organization resembling a network in which authority is determined by knowledge and function. For most of us, this is a new way of thinking about organizational relationships. Displacement of a supreme commander by a multi-agent system of complex interactions is hard for us to imagine. It calls for new vision. We are in transition, learning how to become conscious of emergent order and multi-agent interactions.

As further illustration, consider how Barbara Brown Taylor credits a Newtonian worldview for our structuring of large churches like corporations, "complete with departments, ranked staff members, and organizational charts. Even in churches with congregational polities, the pictures tend to look like pyramids, with straight lines of power that run from top to bottom."[20] Wanting something different, Taylor explains that at one parish where she served she "finally came up with a chart that looked more like a zinnia."[21] Her lay leaders were bewildered by her figure of five concentric circles with the Holy Spirit at the center emanating to a "circle for lay and ordained leaders of the church, with tendrils that reached into the next circle, where all the functioning committees of the church were found. That circle in turn reached into the larger circle of the entire membership of the church, and that circle opened onto the world beyond the church."[22] Taylor was envisioning spheres of influence, not lines of authority, and her lay leaders "wanted to know who was responsible for what and where the buck stopped. Where was the top of this thing, anyway? What do you mean there is not a top, only a center? And why all the porousness between one circle and the next?"[23]

Taylor comments that she understood their frustration, because she too likes following straight lines to get from point A to point B. But her experiences as a pastor forced her to admit that parish ministry is not about getting from point A to point B. Her day regularly included messy interruptions of her best laid plans and "*people* who fouled things up" by showing up unexpectedly with no concern whether she was or was not the right person on the church organizational chart with whom to talk. Parish ministry, Taylor suggests, "was not a journey with a beginning and an end. It was more like a dance, with a lot of wide open space to be explored."[24] Her role was not to construct the best or most orderly plan to get to a particular place on the dance floor. Rather, she came to understand that "A much more promising prospect was to learn how my different partners moved, and to swap as many dance steps with them as I could."[25]

"In other words, there is another way to conceive of our life together. There is another way to conceive of our life in God, too, but it requires a different worldview—not a clockwork universe in which individuals function as discrete springs and gears, but one that looks more like a luminous web, in which the whole is far more than the parts."[26] Emergent change, complex relationships, and heterarchy are ways of thinking that belong to this luminous web.

From Mechanical to Holographic

If a part of the machine is removed, the part neither contains the machine nor is the machine still whole. Similarly, if a piece of a photograph is cut off, say Uncle David's ear, the photograph is missing a part and that piece is a picture of an ear, not of Uncle David.

A hologram, by contrast, is an image in which each part contains the whole. If we were to break off a piece of a hologram, we would have two complete images, but the smaller one would be less well-defined than the larger one. Information is distributed throughout the hologram. Complex phenomena are like a hologram in that they have a necessary unity that cannot be conceptualized in traditional part-whole relations.[27]

The physics of our day demonstrates what David Bohm calls implicate order.[28] This is a kind of order that is more like the order of the hologram. Implicate order occurs throughout the universe where things are not connected in a line as in A → B → C; rather they are interconnected like a web. Schwartz and Ogilvy use the example of a river delta with a network of streams: "It is not possible to predict the flow in any branch of the network of streams in a delta from the flow in the mainstream of the river. The flow in any one branch depends in a complex way on flows in all the other branches."[29] When things are interconnected in this way, a

change in one branch results in adjustments in many or all of the others, but there is no way to determine what will happen in any one particular branch.[30]

From Determinate to Indeterminate

Prediction is the great obsession of science. We try to learn enough about the patterns and conditions surrounding a phenomenon to make it more predictable. One of the most resistant areas in which to make predictions is one that affects us on a daily basis: weather.

We do not understand weather so we have done the next best thing. We measure everything we can about the weather and then we compare it with all the other days when the conditions were the same. If it rained seventy out of one hundred of those days, we say there is a 70 percent chance of rain. We use the same principle when we expect that a new experience will be like the last time we experienced it. We know that these things are not alike in all of their details, but the general pattern holds sufficiently that we can make useful predictions. So why doesn't that seem to work for weather? The answer was discovered by meteorologist Edward Lorenz and is called The Butterfly Effect.

James Gleick describes the significance of Lorenz's 1961 discovery as the disruption that seeded the birth of a new science of seeing order and pattern in what had previously seemed only random chaos.

> With his primitive computer, Lorenz had boiled weather down to the barest skeleton. Yet, line by line, the winds and temperatures in Lorenz's printouts seemed to behave in a recognizable earthly way. They matched his cherished intuition about the weather, his sense that it repeated itself, displaying familiar patterns over time. . . . But the repetitions were never quite exact. There was pattern, with disturbances. An orderly disorder.[31]

One day Lorenz wanted to examine a sequence at greater length. Instead of starting the run over, he started it in the middle by typing in the numbers straight from the printout to restart the initial conditions. He left the room, and when he returned he did not find an exact duplication of the old run. What he found was that the new run departed so far from the old one that the pattern was not recognizable after a time. He discovered that it happened because, "In the computer's memory, six decimal places were stored: .506127. But on the printout, to save space, just three appeared: .506. Lorenz had entered the shorter, rounded-off numbers, assuming that the difference—one part in a thousand—was inconsequential."[32]

Lorenz discovered that weather is unpredictable because it is a complex system. In complex systems small differences may lead to very large changes. This property is called sensitive dependence on initial conditions, or The Butterfly Effect, because the Lorenz attractor generates a computer figure that resembles an owl's eyes or a butterfly's wings.[33]

What became known as The Butterfly Effect grew out of an academic paper he presented in 1972, "Predictability: Does the Flap of a Butterfly's Wings in Brazil Set Off a Tornado in Texas?"[34] As Gleick points out, the idea of the butterfly effect is not new. It appears in folklore:

> For want of a nail, the shoe was lost;
> For want of a shoe, the horse was lost;
> For want of a horse, the rider was lost;
> For want of a rider, the battle was lost;
> For want of a battle, the kingdom was lost![35]

Gleick says that if Lorenz had only seen his data as bad news about weather prediction he would not have planted the seed that led to the new science. Lorenz understood that not only was weather unpredictable and also that unpredictability was necessary. He discovered that there are systems in which small scale intertwines with large. These systems are nonlinear, which means that "the act of playing the game has a way of changing the rules."[36]

From Linear toward Mutual Causality

The most common way to think about causality is "singular causes in a linear and mechanical sequence. Push the rock and it moves. Pushing it again produces the same result."[37]

But newer models of causality describe more complex systems in which there are cycles involving feedback. There is no cause and effect as in $A \rightarrow B$, rather these are mutually causal models $A \leftarrow \rightarrow B$. An example of the difference between these two views of causality can be seen in the change of how we view temperament.

For many years we thought that some babies were born with a bad temperament and that this caused parents to react badly. What we now know is that the more stress parents feel around the birth and early life of a baby, the less they will be able to tolerate difficult babies. The way that stressed parents react to a baby makes the baby's behavior worse, which makes the parents feel more stressed, and so on. It is a cycle of causation with no clear beginning. In this kind of system things change together.

The behavior of such a system is not a result of external control but of feedback. For example, if we shoot a gun at a target, where the bullet hits gives us information (feedback) about how to correct our aim. Norbert Wiener (1894-1964), an American mathematician who established the science of cybernetics, visualized relationships in terms of self-correcting feedback processes in his groundbreaking 1948 book *Cybernetics: or, the Control and Communication in the Animal and the Machine*.[38] Wartime work on radar had prompted Wiener and his assistant Julian Bigelow to look at self-steering mechanisms like thermostats and conclude that feedback is the connection for maintaining order in a disorderly universe. Based on information about the past and forecasts about the future, feedback communicates in the way that brains, autopilots, antiaircraft guns, and thermostats do. In such systems, past output is fed back to the central processor as present input that results in future output. Howard Rheingold summarizes:

> At the beginning of the twentieth century, scientists saw the universe in terms of particles and forces interacting in complicated but orderly patterns that were, in principle, totally predictable. In important ways, all of the nonscientists who lived in an increasingly mechanized civilization also saw the universe in terms of particles and forces and a clockwork cosmos. Around sixty years ago, quantum theory did away with the clockwork and predictability. Around thirty years ago, a few people began to look at the world and see, as Norbert Wiener put it, "a myriad of To Whom It May Concern messages."[39]

Mary Catherine Bateson was influenced by her experience as an eight- or nine-year-old child with a fish tank. Her understanding of her aquarium was informed by the rich imaginative life she inherited from her parents—Margaret Mead and Gregory Bateson—and their friends, and her own interest in Wiener and human adaptation. A thermostat-heater combination regulates temperature in an aquarium through a feedback loop that governs the heater.[40] Negative feedback leads to a change in direction so that the system stays within its preset limits. In the case of a thermostat-heater, when the thermostat detects that the water temperature has passed the limit on the cold side, it causes the heater to turn on. When, as a result of the heater being on, the thermostat detects that the water temperature has passed the limit on the warm side, it causes the heater to turn off.

Schwartz and Ogilvy point out that a system governed by negative feedback tends toward stability. By contrast, positive feedback leads to more of the same direction. If the thermostat in the example above were governed by positive feedback, an increase in temperature would have led to an increase in heat, so that "the temperature went up faster and faster until the glass sides of the tank shattered."[41] Positive feedback loops are part of a cycle of causation with no clear beginning.

Feedback-regulated learning uses dynamic course correction, which is course correction that occurs in real time. The precision of getting it right the first time has a certain appeal, but it is seldom necessary in real life. What we do in most situations is what Seymour Papert refers to as being "vaguely right."[42] That is, we move in a direction and then use feedback to correct our course. This is the way complex systems converge on solutions.

From Assembly toward Morphogenesis

Schwartz and Ogilvy describe the old metaphor for change as a construction project. Before we begin, we have a plan that is developed in detail. Components are gathered and assembled according to the plan, and the outcome is known before the construction begins.

Another kind of change is described as morphogenesis. Through this process, a new, unpredicted and unpredictable form can emerge through the interaction of various interdependent, interacting parts. The new form is constrained by the parts, but not determined by them. Morphogenesis is the metaphor used to describe the emergence of many biological phenomena. "The requirements for morphogenesis are diversity, openness, complexity, mutual causality, and indeterminacy. When these conditions exist, we have the ingredients for qualitative change."[43] The conditions for morphogenetic change are the conditions for emergence.

From Objective toward Perspective

The mind-body distinction can be traced to the Greeks, but in western thought it is the seminal work of René Descartes (1596-1650) that offered the first systematic account of the mind/body dilemma.[44] Scholars to this day continue to argue about the relationship between mind (which included the soul in Descartes' day) and body. "The basic and deceptively simple question is this: Are mind and body—the mental world and the material world—two totally different essences or natures?"[45] Answers to this question have shaped and continue to shape contemporary understandings of mind, body, brain, and consciousness.

Descartes argued that mind and body are qualitatively different. The physical world (matter and body) could be explained by mechanical principles. The nonmaterial rational soul or mind has the capacities of thought and of consciousness that provide us with knowledge of the external world.

By focusing on the problem of true and certain knowledge, Descartes had made epistemology, the question of the relationship between mind and world, the starting point of philosophy. By localizing the soul's contact with body in the pineal gland, Descartes had raised the question of the relationship of mind to the brain and nervous system. Yet at the same time, by drawing a radical ontological distinction between body as extended and mind as pure thought, Descartes, in search of certitude, had paradoxically created intellectual chaos.[46]

Division between subjective (in the mind, soul) and objective (material, uninfluenced by emotions), while still with us, has begun to break down. For many years we have assumed that objective knowledge is more reliable and consistent, perhaps even somehow more true than subjective knowledge. Schwartz and Ogilvy argue that we are beginning to understand that any view is really a perspective. They point to quantum theorist Werner Heisenberg's discovery that, even in physics, the act of observing changes that which is observed: "*Objective* connotes distance from the object of the study; *subjective* connotes a personal view. *Perspective* borrows from both, defining a personal view from some distance. It suggests neither the universality of objectivity nor the personal bias of subjectivity."[47] Perspective acknowledges the role and place of the observer, but keeps some useful distance.[48]

Related to this shift from objective truth to perspective is a shift from the belief that there is a truth that can be found by analysis of the parts. Analysis of the parts is useful in understanding the parts, but it does not help us to understand the wholes. An important aspect of the quest to understand wholes is the shift from the idea of an ultimate singular truth discovered by one best method to a "plurality of kinds of knowledge explored by a multiplicity of approaches."[49] Recognizing the limitations of human life, we have begun to understand that there are many ways to view any real-life situation. We have come to understand that human knowledge is necessarily incomplete and partial.[50] There will inevitably be some level of ambiguity in our knowledge of anything.

How Does This Affect Teaching and Scholarship?

As a culture moves from one set of assumptions to another, the shift is felt in every area of life. Often the shift occurs unevenly across and within disciplines. Perhaps you are already noticing a shift within your discipline and/or across various disciplines? We believe that the seven interrelated features Schwartz and Ogilvy describe provide a powerful context for beliefs about teaching, ourselves as professors, our students, universities and their purposes, and graduate theological education and its purposes, to name a short list.

We are persuaded that we are obliged by our integrity as scholars and professors to examine our assumptions and to become clearer about the ideas underlying our claims. We have used these ideas like a pair of glasses. We look through them to see what we can and to identify views that are most compatible with our other beliefs, using what we can and eliminating the rest. Most of us try on new lenses or ideas with a deep conviction that one day they will be outmoded and that someone, perhaps one of our students, will begin to speak of a new pair of lenses that will allow a new vista to be seen. When that day comes, we hope to be able to try on those new glasses that we bring to our efforts to find new glasses today. We hope we can grow beyond the new ideas we see today as they, in their turn, become old ideas that keep us from seeing yet another vista.

The development of consciousness is an ongoing process, shaped by many personal and cultural factors. In the preface to his commentary on the prophet Jonah, Uriel Simon speaks tellingly of the complex, communal sense of scholarship, and the assumptions that guide and limit its opinions, feeling, and beliefs:

> Each generation produces its own Bible commentaries, in accordance with what it finds perplexing, its exegetical methods, and its emotional and spiritual needs. A generation that shirks its duty of reinterpretaion is shutting its ears to the message that the Bible has to offer. The gates of exegesis are not shut and never will be; each generation has its own special key. . . .[51]

CHAPTER FOUR

Changing Ideas about Learning

Cathedral of Algiers, first Roman labyrinth to convey a Christian meaning.
Its center is a holy text written in a labyrinthine manner. Originated from the Basilica
in Al-Asnam founded in 324. **Courtesy Jeff Saward, photographer.**

"Until we see what is possible, what is appears necessary."

> Jean Piaget (in Sherrie Reynolds, *"Modernism's Devastating Impact on Learning: The Tyranny of Conciousness,"* 2002, 7)

Many of us have experienced academic learning as what one student called cram and release. You may remember making flash cards before an exam in college. We reviewed them every day. Usually, by the night before the exam we had it down to eight to ten cards that we answered incorrectly. By the morning of the exam we had two or three cards left. We took those to the exam, read them right before we walked in, avoided eye contact so that people would know not to speak to us, and prayed that we got the exams right away with no preliminary talking by the professor. As soon as we got a copy of the exam, we wrote the two or three items in pencil on the top of the page.

When we told students about this they laughed and then shared their tricks for learning. We asked them how many of them would get an A on the same exam a week later, or six months later if they took it again. They all agreed that they would probably fail it six months later and might do so one week later. They were baffled when we asked them, "What is the usefulness of that kind of learning?" and "How will that help you in life?" They could not think of a time when the skill of temporarily memorizing large amounts of material would be useful.

When we asked professors the same questions, they did not give much better answers. Some gave a mental muscle explanation, arguing that somehow memorization strengthens the mind. Others expressed faith that memorization had worked for them, so it should work for today's students.

One of our colleagues in the Wabash discussions on learning and teaching at Brite Divinity School expressed appreciation that we had described the way he learns, saying he had never realized before that his students learn that way too. This professor decided to think about changing his teaching to reflect more accurately his own experience of learning:

> I have just completed (January 2004) the Wabash seminar in teaching arranged by professors Toni Craven and Sherrie Reynolds. I realized that there is a serious gap between my own way of learning and the way I teach. In the future I hope to appeal more to what students want to learn, less to what I think they ought to learn. My own learning/research has not been focused on traditional content, but has been intuitive and interest driven. I have done research in Germany, trying to participate in *Auseinandersetzungen* while listening to and speaking German and hearing Latin. I traveled to Jerusalem, visiting early Christian and ancient Jewish

holy places while listening to lectures in Hebrew, discovering zodiacs in synagogue floors that I had not heard about at Yale. Finally, I have twice taken sabbaticals in Rome, learning Italian and suddenly growing interested in [the] Roman domus in Pompeii, later in the aesthetic frescoes on their walls. Especially this third activity is something that few, maybe even no one else in my field is yet doing, but which holds enormous potential for elucidating New Testament texts. My question now is, how can I help my students make such intuitive connections and learn about topics that interest them?[1]

Even though many of us have not explicitly identified our assumptions about how people learn, these assumptions constitute a set of baby elephant beliefs[2] that guide and constrain our teaching. Most of us operate on deeply held, unexamined ideas that were formed during our own undergraduate and graduate education. Without a basis for questioning these ideas and the practices they undergird, we will continue to recreate our own graduate experiences in our current classes. In this chapter, we present a brief history of some of the main turning points in the study of learning and then point to some of the changes that are occurring in the way we now view learning. This tour will be necessarily brief and partial. If it illuminates some of your assumptions and allows you to entertain some ideas that may be new to you, it will have served its purpose.

Modern Learning

The roots of many of our ideas about how people learn can be traced in the story of an interesting series of somewhat serendipitous connections between people and ideas. This intellectual chain extends from Charles Darwin (1809-1882) through Ivan Pavlov (1849-1936) and John Watson (1878-1958) to American behaviorism and B. F. Skinner (1904-1990). Examining this chain reveals the foundation of many currently accepted ideas about how people learn and opens the way, we believe, to some of the new ideas and minority voices from previous periods that are just now beginning to be heard.

Darwinism and Neo-Darwinism

Gerald Holton notes "historians cannot avoid encountering at every turn the primary or secondary effects of certain few extraordinary, transforming works."[3] Holton counts the contribution of the British naturalist Charles Darwin's work among these extraordinary, transforming works. We probably all know at least part of Darwin's story. He was an educated man, conversant with the new ideas of his day in a variety of fields of study. A naturalist, he was trained to observe carefully. On his voyage on the HMS *Beagle*, he made detailed notes of his observations and "a sketch of the conclusions," which he claimed, "seemed to me probable."[4]

Darwin's ideas on evolution were first published in 1845 as his *Journal of Researches During HMS* Beagle's *Voyage Round the World.* His most famous work, *On the Origin of Species by Means of Natural Selection, or the Preservation of Favoured Races in the Struggle for Life* (usually referred to as *The Origin of Species*), appeared in 1859.

Darwin's theory did not, of course, specify a mechanism for evolution, since Mendel's landmark paper was not read until 1865. The later extension of Darwin's ideas that included genes as the mechanism of evolution is called Neo-Darwinism, and it is in this form that the theory has been most influential. Neo-Darwinism is "the theory that evolution is brought about by natural selection based on random genetic mutations."[5]

Darwin established a basis for research on animals to be used as a way to understand humans. According to Julian Huxley, *The Origin of Species* marked a change in the "entire picture of man and his place and role in nature."[6] Darwin's principle of natural selection was so powerful and fit so well with the tenor of the times that it influenced how we think about biological, intellectual, and social change.

Darwin believed that nature produces an abundance from which natural selection winnows out the best. This idea found its way into behavioral psychology as the notion that organisms (animals and people) emit behaviors from which the environment selects the behaviors best suited to it. Both are adaptive processes in which an organism adapts to an environment that is making demands upon it.

These two ideas, using animals to study human psychological events and learning as an adaptive process, came together in the work of Ivan Pavlov on Classical Conditioning.

Ivan Pavlov (1849-1936)

Ivan Pavlov was born in a small village in Russia. His family hoped he would become a priest, and he attended seminary for a time. It was after reading Darwin's work that he decided he was more interested in science than theology, and he left seminary to study at the University of St. Petersburg.[7] Pavlov was awarded the Nobel Prize in medicine in 1904 for his work on digestion, but the work for which he is best known was a curious side-note to this original study.

His research on digestion in dogs was conducted by externalizing the salivary glands in dogs so that he could measure the amount of saliva produced in response to food under different conditions. Pavlov noticed that the dogs produced saliva before the food actually touched their mouths. This observation changed the direction of his subsequent research. He conducted a long series of experiments in which he studied saliva produced in the presence of a number of different stimuli prior to the presentation of food. "He thereby established the basic laws for the establishment and extinction of what he called conditional reflexes—i.e. reflex responses, like salivation, that only occurred conditional upon specific previous experiences of the animal. These experiments were carried out in the 1890s and 1900s, and were known to western scientists through translations of individual accounts, but first became fully available in English in a book published in 1927."[8]

The essence of the process that Pavlov called conditional reflex and which later was translated as conditioned reflex, was to explain how food-related behavior occurs in the presence of stimuli that are reliably associated with food. Those of us with pets may notice, for example, that the sound of a can opener brings the dog or cat running to the kitchen in anticipation of being fed.[9] While Pavlov advised caution in extending his research to cognition, he also said, "It is obvious that the different kinds of habits based on training, education and discipline of any sort are nothing but a long chain of conditioned reflexes."[10]

Pavlov saw parallels between internal, cognitive processes and the physiological events he had studied. In fact, in his acceptance speech for the Nobel Prize, he said, "In a word, the experiments with psychical stimulation prove to be exact, but miniature, models of the experiments with physiological stimulations by the same substances."[11]

This was an important breakthrough, making it possible to study psychological events through their physiological manifestations. To this day, people tend to lend more credibility to claims that appear to have a physiological basis, even if those claims violate our experience and other accumulated wisdom.

John Broadus Watson (1878-1958)

The next important link in the intellectual chain of modernism's ideas about learning is John Broadus Watson. Born to a poor family in the rural town of Travelers Rest, South Carolina, Watson's father was described as "lazy and delinquent" and his mother as "religious." Watson's father left the family when Watson was thirteen.[12]

Watson was a mediocre student at Furman University, earning some of his lowest grades in his psychology classes. There is a story about a philosophy professor who told students that if they turned a paper in "backward" they would risk failing the course. Watson took the challenge and the professor failed him, causing Watson to remain at Furman for another year.

When Watson's mother died, he changed his major from ministry to philosophy. He was the youngest person to earn a Ph.D. at the University of Chicago, graduating *magna cum laude* and Phi Beta Kappa. He studied philosophy with John Dewey but said he "didn't understand the man," and chose as his major professor a psychologist named James Rowland Angell instead.

Watson had a successful fourteen-year career at Johns Hopkins, which was cut short when he was asked to resign following an affair with a research assistant. After he resigned from Johns Hopkins, the academic community ostracized Watson, although he continued to be honored for his contributions to psychology. For the remainder of his life, he worked in advertising.

In 1913, Watson saw the possibility of using Pavlov's ideas to "develop techniques whereby he could condition and control the emotions of human subjects."[13] This led to his best known and often criticized experiment (conducted with the help of the research assistant with whom he had the relationship that later cost him his Hopkins position and later his marriage). The study, which was unethical by today's standards, is known as the "Little Albert Study," after the eleven-month-old baby named Albert who was the subject of the experiment. Watson presented a white rat and a loud noise to Little Albert. After several pairings, Albert showed fear of the white rat. Later, Albert generalized the fear to stimuli that were similar to the rat, such as a beard.

Watson began a revolution, calling for psychology (and the study of learning) to become "a totally objective psychology—a science of behavior—dealing only with observable behavioral acts that could be objectively described in terms of stimulus and response."[14]

Watson, considered the founder of behaviorism, believed that the study of animals could be extended to the study of humans. He acknowledged that humans were more complex than animals, but he believed that the basic underlying principles were the same. "All animals, he believed, were extremely complex machines that responded to situations according to their 'wiring', or nerve pathways that were conditioned by experience."[15] The adoption of objective psychology spelled the end of introspection as a way of understanding psychological events. Psychology was to be studied using the same methods as physiology, reducing the study of interior experience to that which can be described by an outside observer. Such a reduction fit well with the values and goals of the modern period.

B. F. Skinner (1904-1990)

Burrhus Frederic Skinner is perhaps the best known and most influential of the behaviorists who followed after Pavlov and Watson. An American, Skinner was born in Susquehanna, Pennsylvania. According to his elder daughter, Julie Vargas, he spent much of his boyhood building things, "for example a cart with steering that worked backwards (by mistake) and a perpetual motion machine (the latter did not work). Other ventures were more successful."[16]

Skinner graduated from college with a degree in English and lived in Greenwich Village in New York for a while. While working in a bookstore as a clerk and writing a few papers, he serendipitously came upon books by Pavlov and Watson and became intrigued. When he returned to graduate school, he earned a master's and doctorate in psychology.

His mentor at Harvard, William Crozier, chair of physiology, "fervently adhered to a program of studying the behavior of 'the animal as a whole' without appealing, as the psychologists did, to processes going on inside. That exactly matched Skinner's goal of relating behavior to experimental conditions."[17] Vargas also reports that Skinner managed to complete his work at Harvard with "each department, psychology and physiology," assuming "the other was supervising the young student." In fact, Skinner claimed he was "'doing exactly as I pleased.'"[18]

Skinner was inventing devices, just as he had done as a boy, but now he was creating devices for use in experiments. His daughter writes,

> After a dozen pieces of apparatus and some lucky accidents (described in his "A Case History in Scientific Method"), Skinner invented the cumulative recorder, a mechanical device that recorded every response as an upward movement of a horizontally moving line. The slope showed rate of responding. This recorder revealed the impact of the contingencies over responding. Skinner discovered that the rate with which the rat pressed the bar depended not on any preceding stimulus (as Watson and Pavlov had insisted), but on what followed the bar presses. This was new indeed. Unlike the reflexes that Pavlov had studied, this kind of behavior operated on the environment and was controlled by its effects. Skinner named it operant behavior. The process of arranging the contingencies of reinforcement responsible for producing this new kind of behavior he called operant conditioning.[19]

The behaviorists realized that Pavlov's reflexes could not be the foundation for all that we learn. Human babies learn prodigious amounts in early life, which could not all be elaborated from the small set of inborn reflexes. Based on Sigmund Freud's idea that humans are motivated to seek pleasure and avoid pain, Skinner proposed that people emit behaviors and those that are rewarded become more likely to be repeated in the future. Skinner became America's leading behaviorist and one of the most powerful influences on the way we view learning.[20] *as external event*

The September 20, 1971, *Time* magazine cover featured Skinner with the caption, *"We Can't Afford Freedom."* Skinner is noted for important distinctions regarding freedom:

> Personal freedom also seems threatened. It is only the feeling of freedom, however, which is affected. Those who respond because their behavior has had positively reinforcing consequences usually feel free. They seem to be doing what they want to do. Those who respond because the reinforcement has been negative and who are therefore avoiding or escaping from punishment are doing what they have to do and do not feel free. These distinctions do not involve the fact of freedom.[21]

Turning Points in Modern and Post-Modern Ideas of Learning

A turning point between modern views of learning and post-modern views is found in the learning theories of the Swiss scholar Jean Piaget (1896-1980) and the Russian Lev Vygotsky (1896-1934). Piaget described learning as self-organizing, establishing that learning is an internal event that may be triggered, but not caused by something in the environment. Vygotsky situated learning in the larger culture, pioneering the notion that intellectual development is a function of human communities, rather than individuals. Piaget and Vygotsky did not agree on everything, but they were in agreement on many issues, and certainly were in more agreement with each other than either was with behaviorism.

Jean Piaget (1896-1980)

Jean Piaget was born in Neuchâtel, Switzerland, in 1896. At age eleven, Piaget wrote a short paper on an albino sparrow, which is generally considered as the start of his brilliant scientific career during which he authored over ninety-five books and six hundred articles. He was also a well-known malacologist, writing noted studies of mollusks in his late adolescence. Piaget studied natural sciences at the University of Neuchâtel where he obtained a Ph.D. He spent one year working at L'écôle de la rue de la Grange-aux-Belles in France (a school for boys created by Alfred Binet and then directed by Théodore Simon who had developed with Binet a test for the measurement of intelligence).

In 1923, Piaget and Valentine Châtenay were married. The couple had three children, Jacqueline, Lucienne, and Laurent, whose intellectual development from infancy to language was much studied by Piaget.

Successively or simultaneously, Piaget occupied several chairs: psychology, sociology, and history of science; history of scientific thinking; the International

Bureau of Education; psychology and sociology; sociology, then genetic and experimental psychology from 1940 to 1971. In 1955, he created and directed until his death the International Center for Genetic Epistemology.

Piaget's interest in evolution and his work with the psychologist Alfred Binet led him to propose the evolution of thought in children as a model for the evolution of thought over the course of human history. Piaget believed that behavioral adaptation occurs in both pre-intelligent and intelligent forms. In early life (of the individual and the species), we rely on instinct and habit. Piaget saw habit as individually acquired instincts. These are, of course, very limited forms of knowledge in that certain contingencies set them off and they proceed in automatic sequence. Intention and intelligence are not involved.

A later form of adaptation, which he calls sensorimotor and semiotic-operational, is intelligent adaptation, allowing mistakes to be corrected and responses to be changed. The ultimate form of this intelligent adaptation is the ability to manipulate symbolic models of a situation so that mistakes can be corrected before they occur. Intelligence, in Piaget's view, is what allows evolution to proceed in ways that result in bad ideas dying rather than in genomic evolution alone, where bad genetic ideas result in the death of the organism. The mechanism underlying this evaluation of ideas is what Piaget called equilibration, which is an internal drive for knowledge that leads a person to transform her/his forms of knowledge, therefore improving them.

Equilibration is a process whereby we form an initial idea, then elaborate and add to this idea until at some point we become aware of gaps, inconsistencies, and contradictions in it. This is the point where the idea disequilibrates. When you and we were students it sometimes felt like we came to a time in the semester when we had to find a new way of organizing and conceptualizing material so that it had more coherence and made more sense. We always hoped that we did not get to that place right before an exam, because it felt as if we were between ways of thinking about the material.

Piaget says that in the face of disequilibration we try to find a new way of thinking that eliminates the gaps, contradictions, and inconsistencies. As we use this newly equilibrated idea, we add to it and elaborate until at some point we become aware of gaps, inconsistencies, and contradictions in it, and the process continues.

This process of development, Piaget believes, underlies the differences between the ways children think and the ways adults think. By adolescence, children and adults are all capable of what he called formal reasoning, which is the ability to hypothesize, to reason, to isolate and test variables, and the like.

It would be nice if humans progressed in such a tidy fashion so that we could count on the fact that all of our students were able to reason in this way, but it has not been our experience. In fact, Piaget's theory only predicts that students are capable of formal reasoning; whether they reason formally depends on the experiences they have had and especially the kind of problems they have tried to solve. Maturation alone is not enough. This means that we can expect a variety of approaches and thought processes among our students, including some that are reminiscent of much younger people.

Piaget did not study the developmental processes of university students or adults. However, subsequent researchers have done so. William Perry (1999) in a book first published in 1968, developed a view of university learning by combining Piaget's ideas with a thorough study of Harvard undergraduates.[22] Barbara Hursh, Paul Haas, and Michael Moore extended Piaget's concept of centration, which originally described the tendency of young children to focus on a single aspect or dimension of an object. They discussed cognitive decentering in college students as "the intellectual capacity to move beyond a single center of focus . . . and consider a variety of other perspectives in a coordinated way to perceive reality more accurately, process information more systematically, and solve problems more effectively."[23] The term decentering, in this context, denotes the ability to shift deliberately among alternative perspectives or frames of reference and to bring them to bear upon each other or upon a problem at hand.[24]

Lev Semyonovich Vygotsky (1896-1934)

Lev Vygotsky was born in northern Russia to a middle-class Jewish family. He was one of eight children. His father was a banking executive and his mother, a licensed teacher. Because of discrimination against Jews, Vygotsky's early education was provided by a private tutor who dialogued with him in questions and answers. Vygotsky later attended a private prep school, where he excelled in mathematics and classical studies, became proficient in languages, and developed a keen interest in literature, theater, and poetry.

Vygotsky wanted to study literature, but because that would lead to a degree in teaching, which was prohibited to him because of his religion, he enrolled in medical school. He simultaneously enrolled in another university to study literature and graduated from both in 1917, the year of the Russian Revolution. One of Vygotsky's most famous students, Aleksandr R. Luria, explains that prior to the revolution there were strictly divided classes in Russia. The revolution changed this and created a period of unparalleled freedom and action in Russian society. Luria says, "The limits of our restricted, private world were broken down by the Revolution, and new vistas opened before us. We were swept up in a great historical movement. Our private interests were consumed by the wider social goals of a new, collective society."[25] Though his life was cut short in 1934 by tuberculosis, Vygotsky wrote prolifically. Shortly after his death his writings were banned and his name was removed from scientific journals by the Stalinist regime. Fortunately, his family kept his numerous manuscripts safe. In 1956, his daughter, Gita Vygotsky, began to have them translated and published.

These manuscripts, written in the 1920s and 1930s, were based on his belief that psychology was in a state of crisis. Pavlov and others had succeeded in establishing a material basis for elementary psychological processes but had no adequate method for describing some of the traditional concerns of psychology such as voluntary memory, abstract problem solving, and creative imagination. These were previously studied by introspective, verbal methods that had been rejected by behaviorism.

Vygotsky argued that human thought and learning cannot be understood only in terms of biological adaptation. The chain of thought that began with Pavlov that had reduced human thought to physiology began to be reversed with Vygotsky. Vygotsky established that human nature is more than our physiological heritage; it is also our culture, the tools we have developed, and the ways we interact with each other.

Vygotsky, like Piaget, believed that people construct their own knowledge. He extended a tenet of Marxism that "the animal merely uses external nature, and brings about changes in it simply by his presence; man by his changes makes it serve his ends, masters it. This is the final, essential distinction between man and other animals."[26] Vygotsky extended this idea of tools to include symbolic tools. Both kinds of tools are created by human societies and change over time.[27]

Vygotsky believed that younger people use older people as one of the tools in developing their mental processes and knowledge. Through interaction with older people, younger ones learn about their culture, their history, and the ways that their culture has learned to deal with environments. Vygotsky also believed that learning is driven by the need to make meaning, to make sense of things, not by survival instincts alone.

Vygotsky held that the transition periods in learning were important. For him, it is not enough to determine what a person knows; one must also determine what a person is able to learn. For Vygotsky, as for Piaget, there are important differences between two people who are performing at a certain level if one of them is in transition. The person in transition is about to be on the next level. For Vygotsky, this means that "you must do more than just test . . . you must interact with him, give him clues, teach him, then see if he has caught on."[28] Riever points out that this is similar to the anthropologist Gregory Bateson's (1904-1980) idea that "something is being grasped in the usual way, but something else is also being learnt, something that in short order will bootstrap cognition up to the next level."[29]

Post-Modern Learning

Learning in the post-modern world is about relation, pattern, and form. In this new view, mind is many layered, recursive, and related to the external environment in mutually causal ways. In part, thanks to Vygotsky and Piaget, learning is no longer viewed as something caused from the outside. We now find it more useful to think of learning as constructed, self-organizing, and self-regulating. There is more room here for the messy kind of learning characterized by spurts and gaps. It allows for the surprises and seemingly random connections and for the dynamic bubbling up or emergence of ideas that form themselves into relationships.

Learning through Feedback

One of the key ideas in this new view of learning is the idea of feedback. Feedback-regulated learning creates a recursive modification of thought and dynamic course correction that in 1993 Papert called pilotage.[30] It is similar to the way one pilots a boat by heading in a particular direction, taking measurements, and correcting the course en route. The precision of getting it right the first time has a certain appeal, but it is very seldom used in real life, and is very seldom necessary in real life. What most of us do in most situations is what Papert refers to as being vaguely right. That is, we move in a direction and then use feedback to correct our course.

One of us (SR) was once involved in a robotics project that included our studying expert systems, which simulate intelligence through a computer program. The project was to get a robot to walk in a door and around a room. The program worked well, but when we tried to use it to govern a real robot, it was a disaster. In real life,

relate to assessment process

movements are not so precise, and when the robot took a step that was a little longer or shorter, when it turned at an angle slightly more or less than the one specified, this small initial error was magnified until at the end of the simple exercise it was walking into a wall. Real life is messier than life in the virtual world. In real life, pilotage works better than trying to create the entire design before taking the first step.

One of the legacies of behaviorism is the notion that making errors may lead to the errors being strengthened so that learning environments are to be designed to minimize errors. In behaviorism there is a premium for getting it right the first time. On the other hand, Piaget believed that errors are a necessary part of learning. In Piaget's theory, it is error that allows a person's ideas to correct themselves in light of experience. When an idea does not work out as we expect, the surprise leads us to re-think it. Where behaviorism strives to eliminate error, pilotage expects and makes use of error as a means of self-correction.

Learning Is Self-Organizing

Piaget argued that learning is not caused by teaching or by any outside influence.[31] The mind does not regulate its learning in response to environmental pressure, but to achieve coherence or to reduce dissonance. In 1987, Humberto R. Maturana and Francisco J. Varela arrived at a similar idea by a very different path. They are biologists who were studying vision. They discovered that they could better account for vision by assuming a "view from the inside" than by traditional views.[32] Traditional theories account for vision as a stimulus that enters the eye and is passed along the optic system to the brain. The radical change Maturana and Varela made was to think of the experience of seeing as something created by the nervous system rather than as an image relayed by the nervous system. They argue that the experience of vision is created by the nervous system, which is why hallucinations seem so real. They maintain that the entire nervous system is self-organizing, a process they named autopoiesis in 1973.[33] The nervous system responds to an internal need for coherence rather than an external cause. Learning is similarly constructed by the mind.

No outside event can cause learning. At best it can create conditions to which the learner will respond, but the nature of the response cannot be determined ahead of time, and is not determined by the conditions, events, words, or other stimuli. This is a clear and radical departure from traditional views of mind and learning.

The environment is no longer viewed as causing learning or as leading inevitably to a particular idea or set of ideas. The outside world does not impinge on the learner. We can no longer assume that we are objective, outside observers. As Alfred Korzybski suggests, we do not directly observe and describe the world. We construct ideas about the world and we do so in words. This is a mapping process, and Korzybski cautions us, "the map is not the territory."[34]

On the other hand, Peter Harries-Jones says the map is not the result of some random process. "The map is not the territory, but a correct map must have a similar structure to the territory. This accounts for its usefulness. If the structures are similar, then the empirical world becomes 'rational' to a potentially rational being."[35] The renowned physicist, Stephen Hawking, holds that "one cannot say what time actually is. All one can do is describe what has been found to be a good mathematical model for time and say what predictions it makes."[36] Fortunately, the maps we construct are good enough in most cases to be useful. But the relationship between our verbal world and the external environment may no longer be considered direct.

Maturana and Varela liken this relationship between the verbal world and the external environment to a person who has always lived in a submarine. From the outside, an observer sees changes in the submarine with respect to reefs, water surface, and the like. But "all that exists for the man inside the submarine are indicator readings, their transitions, and ways of obtaining specific relations between them."[37]

Post-modern thought recognizes that a person's environment consists as much of stories as anything else. We do not have direct contact with reality. The environment is not just what it is, but what we say it is and what we are told it is. Narratives guide our actions and interactions and perhaps, our feelings. In 1991, Eisner said, "The eye is not only a part of the brain, it is a part of tradition."[38]

The narratives and guiding metaphors that constitute an individual's perspective determine the world in which she or he lives. Individual narratives are, of course, interwoven with, and partially made up of, remnants of family, sub-cultural, and cultural narratives. Jill Freedman and Gene Combs describe the way realities are socially constructed. They talk about an imaginary situation in which two survivors of some disaster come together to start a new society. As the two begin to coordinate their activities for survival they agree on certain habits, distinctions, and ultimately language. The original two people will remember that these are agreements, but for the children of this generation, the agreements will be referred to as " 'This is how our elders do it,' and by the third generation it will be 'this is how it is done'. . . . By the fourth generation of our imaginary society, 'This is how it is done' will have become 'This is the way the world is; this is reality.' "[39]

Importance of Unconscious Thought in Learning

Modern thought has privileged conscious thought and intention and marginalized unconscious, dream, vision, intuition, and imagination, much to our detriment. Gregory Bateson argues that unconscious thought is qualitatively different from conscious thought. He describes consciousness as linear, partial, and selective. It deals in description, classification, and comparison. Unconscious thought is the global. It is the primary means of experiencing relationships between self and others and self and environment. Referring to Korzybki's distinction, Bateson says that in unconscious thought map and territory are equated, whereas conscious thought deals only with the map.[40]

The unconscious is both a source of thought and a repository for it. As an economy of thought, we sink habits to the level of the unconscious. Such habits may be actions, thoughts, or beliefs that are familiar and repetitive. Eventually they seem like second nature to us, like the way things are, like a part of us. We no longer examine or consider them.

The unconscious is not just a repository, though. It is also a rich source of thought, dream, vision, and imagination. It is, as Bateson suggested, the source of our direct experience of ourselves and our world. It is where, as phenomenologist Robert Romanyshyn said, "The universe would speak through me."[41]

It is this notion of unconscious that has been most neglected, and even treated with suspicion in the modern era. The combination of modern skepticism toward anything that is not directly observable, the privileging of conscious, intentional thought, and the Freudian view of the unconscious' participation in pathology have combined to distance us from this rich and ancient way of knowing.

However, some of the greatest scientific thinkers of our time have relied on imagination, dream, and an inner sense of resonance and aesthetics. Albert Einstein's theory of relativity was in part a result of his thought experiment in which he wondered what it would be like to ride on a wave of light. Mandelbrot's fractal geometry came to him first in a dream.

Richard Feynman tells the story of his early days as a physics professor at Cornell University. He had been working very hard in his lab and was not coming up with any new ideas or solutions. He had decided he was burned out. He says, "They expect me to accomplish something, and I can't accomplish anything! I have no ideas."[42] Later, as he thought back, he realized that he used to enjoy physics. He played with it and had fun with it. "I used to do whatever I felt like doing—it didn't have to do with whether it was important for the development of nuclear physics, but whether it was interesting and amusing for me to play with."[43]

Feynman reports that within a week of recovering this playful attitude, he was walking through a cafeteria. He saw someone throwing a plate into the air. Feynman noticed something in the way the plate wobbled that interested him. He set about trying to understand it just because he was curious. It was hard to see how understanding the wobble of a plate could be useful to nuclear physics, but it was the beginning of the idea that led to his Nobel Prize.

Learning as Emergent Order

Emergent order is one of the delights of learning. The experience of elements of an idea coming together into a new coherence is one of the great satisfactions of human life. Scholars and poets alike know that this kind of ordering cannot be forced and does not occur on a timetable. The best we can do is to have a prepared mind. To wait, as a faculty member once said, "Until the muse in my mind opens the door and is willing to share her wisdom."

We suggest that it is useful to think of learning as a fundamental, unconscious process of sensing relationships, redundancy, difference, and pattern. We can, and do, act on this sense of things, but because much of our learning depends upon social networks, we often need to translate what we are learning into a form that can be shared with others. Consciousness does not produce knowledge; rather, as Brent Davis, Dennis J. Sumara, and Rebecca Luce-Kapler note: "Well before we become aware of a perception or thought, complex nonconscious processes have sorted through and discarded information so that what enters consciousness has already been selected and has already been rendered meaningful."[44]

Robert Quinn tells the story of an interview with a CEO about the first five years of the company.

It was an impressive story about the unfolding of a clear strategic plan. He described the company as moving effortlessly from phase A to B and then to C. This account did not match my understanding of what had taken place. I interjected and described a very different history. When he was challenged with the actual chaotic learning process that had taken place, he paused and then smiled and said, "It's true, we built the bridge as we walked on it."[45]

Organizational and personal growth seldom follows a linear plan. This is an important principle to remember. When people recount a history of growth, they often tell it in a linear sequence, suggesting a rationality and control that never really existed.

We have developed standards for shared knowledge that avoid some of the idiosyncratic errors in thought. We subject shared knowledge to public scrutiny and debate. This very human process can be used in teaching in a similar way. In the course of conversation, students hear other, more adequate or elegant ways to think about or solve a problem. Students who are encouraged to work together, to consult with one another, to expose their ideas to public scrutiny, and to make use of the feedback they receive are learning skills that will be useful to them throughout life. Unfortunately, we have so separated everyday knowledge from academic, public knowledge that many students find the gap un-crossable. Some of them simply view academic knowledge as a kind of game that one plays to get a degree and a job.

Some students assume that the experts are right and distance themselves from their own inner sense of things. One of us (SR) saw this graphically in a class once where she was trying to provide students with an opportunity to think about some mathematical ideas differently. She provided them with a table full of paper, rulers, string, scissors, cups, and everything else she could imagine that might be useful. She asked them to find the volume of a cone (actually of a particular cone represented by a paper cup). One student didn't pick up anything from the table, but just sat back with a very dejected look on her face. She stayed that way for so long that I (SR) went over and asked her what was the matter. She said, "I've failed." I pointed out that she hadn't failed yet, since she had not yet tried anything. She said, "I can't remember the formula."

For her, the formula was not a means of expressing relationships, it was something to memorize and recall. Without the recollection, she did not have any idea how to begin to think about the problem.

We have reduced mind to a fraction of what it is and can be. Certainly, we have under-utilized the unconscious. Perhaps as we reclaim these neglected aspects of mind we will re-engineer the conditions we create to foster learning. We hope that we will recognize that learning and reporting on learning are two different functions, occurring in vastly different ways. We have created the conditions to support conscious reporting on learning. Now perhaps we will attend to the need to create rich conditions necessary for the unconscious development of learning to occur.

CHAPTER FIVE

Changing Ideas about Curriculum

Turf Labyrinth, Snienton, England. **Courtesy Jeff Saward, photographer.**

"Following a Wittgensteinian path, meaning is conveyed and transformed
through language and our creative invention of ideas."

M. Jayne Fleener (*Curriculum Dynamics: Recreating Heart*, 2002, 11)

The teacher-scholar model guarantees that we who teach are also among those
who extend the reach of knowledge into the darkness. We know the flaws and
limitations of human knowledge, which is always, by its nature, incomplete
and partial. We know the flaws and inadequacies of the work that has been done
and, on a good day, we know that it is useful anyway.

Early in our teaching we assumed that our students were like us. We thought
they would also find our disciplines fascinating and that they would be persuaded by
the careful ways in which research had been conducted. Over the years we discovered
how wrong we were. Our students have a variety of reasons for enrolling in our
classes. Students are not, it turns out, as interested as we are in our disciplines.

Curriculum as Sequence

We believed, without real evidence, that there was a necessary order in the material
to be taught. We designed courses to lead the class from point A to point B. Early on,
we thought of courses as sets of ideas that students must learn. Later we thought of
teaching as sets of experiences coupled with ideas that students would use to form
their own ideas and beliefs. In both cases, we had the sense that students approached
courses as something to get through or what our TCU colleague, David Grant, calls
chit gathering.

William Doll, one of the foremost post-modern curriculum theorists, points out
that the Latin word *curriculum* literally "means either 'a course for running' or a
'chariot for racing' such a course (*A Comprehensive Etymological Dictionary of the
English Language,* s.v. curriculum)."[1] Doll writes that the idea of learning in
sequential order did not occur until Peter Ramus (Petrus Ramus in Latin, Pierre de
la Ramée in French), a sixteenth-century contemporary of John Calvin and master at
the University of Paris, gave us his map of curriculum in 1576.[2] From that point, in
just about four centuries, we have seen curriculum as set before the teaching
begins, our lesson plans of material to be covered are devised prior to, not after, our
teaching (except, of course, for those teachers who cheat). Ramus's new methodol-
ogy—a taxonomic, hierarchical ordering from general to the particular in a linear,
unbroken progression—was denounced by his colleagues as a vulgar short-cut, which
diluted the ancient and noble profession of dialogue.[3]

A Ramist Map

TABVLA ARTIVM, QVAS IN
hoc Volumine coniunximus.

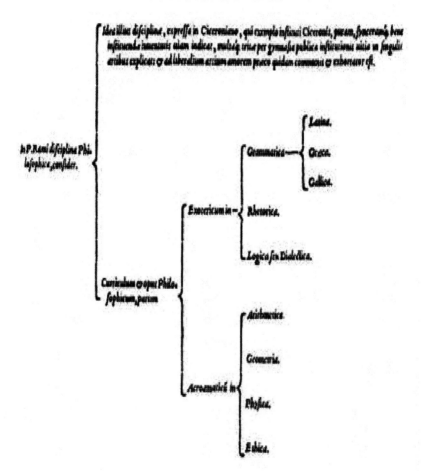

Source: P. Ramus, *Professio regia*, Basle, 1576.

In an interesting side note, Doll points out that the idea that food should be eaten in courses and served in a particular order occurred at about the same time. It may be that the idea of order emerged as a more pervasive cultural trend, rather than only a curricular trend.[4] In the Middle Ages, "Learning and teaching occurred when groups of itinerant students gathered at the feet of the master to study a text or texts with the resplendent glosses the master chose or wrote himself. Pupils wandered from master to master and from city to city, 'studying' as long as they wished. There was no sense of sequence to this process or of one ever having 'finished.'"[5]

In the workplace, Comte de Saint-Simon, "father of technocracy and premiere theoretician of industrialism," introduced ideas of efficient production, scientific decision making, and orderly behavior.[6] The idea was developed in America by Frederick Taylor's scientific management of workers at the Bethlehem Steel Company in the 1890s. Doll points out that at the time "it was common for day laborers to work in groups under the direction of a foreman. Decisions were made collectively or sometimes through default by the laziest worker."[7] Taylor introduced a new method, and increased productivity and efficiency that formulated four duties or principles to which management needed to pay attention. First, a science for each element of a man's work must be developed to replace the old rule-of-thumb method. Second, the workmen must be scientifically selected and trained, not left to their own methods, as was done in the past. Third, attention must be given "to insure all of the work being done in accordance with the principles . . . developed." Fourth, "an equal division of the work and the responsibility must be drawn between management and the workmen."[8]

Management's task, Doll says, was to plan in advance what each worker was to do. Each worker was to receive these detailed plans in writing each day. "These orders specify 'not only what is to be done but how it is to be done and the exact time allowed for doing it.' This pre-ordering of tasks, by managers for workers is the most prominent single element in modern scientific management."[9]

Doll points out that the belief that the task should be pre-ordered by management "assumes that ends should be fixed prior to the implementation of means. Efficiency, then, is measured in terms of the number of specific ends achieved and the time needed for achievement. Such a linear and closed system tends to trivialize the goals of education, limiting them to only that which can be particularized."[10]

These beliefs, Doll proposes, "flourished most in those geographical areas 'tinged by Calvinism'—Germany and the Netherlands. Hence, there was an affinity between the discipline, order, and control Calvin felt all Christians should bring to their lives and that which Ramus brought to pedagogy." Calvinist universities were the first to adopt the idea of curriculum as a set course to be followed and finished.[11]

The idea that there is *a* structure to knowledge and a direct relation between this structure and the way knowledge is acquired "has done immense damage to pedagogy and curriculum theory."[12] We are now aware that knowledge can be structured in many ways, depending on the purpose, context, and people doing the structuring.

With Piaget and Vygotsky, we also know that learning is more likely to occur during the self-structuring of knowledge than in the receiving of knowledge already structured by someone else.[13] Learning is related to the psychological processes of knowledge construction as well as the logical structure of a body of knowledge, not one or the other alone.

Mathematics and science have influenced our understanding of ourselves and our world in subtle ways, according to one of Doll's colleagues, M. Jayne Fleener. She says that, "the curriculum hierarchy both reflects the importance of the mathematization of reality as a fundamental paradigm of modernity and emphasizes the consequences of the conceptual framework upon which the scientific paradigm is based."[14] Fleener notes that the "underlying logic of the scientific method is fundamentally hegemonic, creating an imbalance in ways of knowing, emphasizing and elevating the status of scientific rationality over other forms of knowing."[15]

Post-Modern Curriculum

A post-modern curriculum is a curriculum that recognizes the complexity of teaching and learning and creates conditions for learning that honors this complexity. The recognition of complex phenomena is relatively new.[16] The new sciences of complexity are loosely bound together by the belief that some phenomena are complex and require a different science to understand them. Traditional analytical methods of modern science work well for simple and what Paul Cilliers calls complicated systems. The problems arise when such methods are used to study systems that are complex.

Cilliers clearly describes the difference between complex and complicated:

> Some systems have a very large number of components and perform sophisticated tasks, but in a way that can be analyzed (in the full sense of the word) accurately. Such a system is complicated. Other systems are constituted by such intricate sets of non-linear relationships and feedback loops that only certain aspects of them can be analyzed at a time. Moreover, these analyses would always cause distortions. Systems of this kind are complex.[17]

A complex system is composed of a great many independent agents that interact with each other in a great many ways.

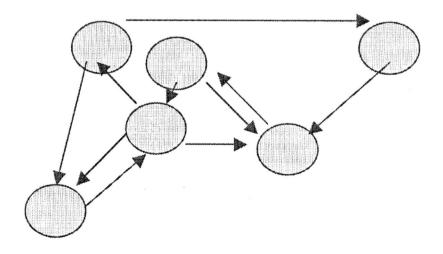

The richness of the interactions allows the system as a whole to undergo spontaneous self-organization. *detecting patterns, relation, form p. 38*

Cilliers offers the following list of characteristics of complex systems:[18]

- Large number of elements

- Elements interact dynamically

- "Interaction is fairly rich, i.e., any element in the system influences and is influenced by quite a few other ones."

- Have a history

- "Each element in the system is ignorant of the behaviour of the system as a whole, it responds only to information that is available to it locally."

Classes are better described as complex rather than complicated or simple. A large (in system terms) number of independent agents are interacting in dynamic, real time. The interaction is rich in the sense that, when students participate, the ideas they express spark ideas for others or change others' views. Even when they are not encouraged to speak, classes can be conceptualized in terms of the rich interactions within each student, between their history (personal and intellectual), texts, the professor, material from other classes, and interactions with others outside of class. That is a very rich environment indeed. Classes have a history, and they quickly develop a culture and character, adding to their complexity. Each element, student and professor, is   s acting on local information, within the class.

Knowledge is complex in many of the same ways and for many of the same reasons. Our processes of generating knowledge create an illusion of simplicity and certainty. We do not agree with other theories and people in our field about what is true or even what is important. All of this complexity must be honored in our teaching.

Cilliers cites Jean-Francois Lyotard's 1974 classic, *The Postmodern Condition*, in which Lyotard says that the shift from modern to postmodern thought is characterized, in part, by an "incredulity toward meta-narratives."[19]

Instead of looking for a simple discourse that can unify all forms of knowledge, we have to cope with a multiplicity of discourses, many different language games—all of which are determined locally, not legitimated externally. Different institutions and different contexts produce different narratives which are not reducible to each other.[20]

When we represent knowledge by single, seamless narratives, we obscure complexity. Creating space for the discussion of different perspectives and treating the mainstream narrative as one of several ways this topic might be constructed, rather than as the way the topic *should* be constructed, seems more profitable. We might point out the gaps, inconsistencies, and contradictions in our discipline. We might make space for as many voices and perspectives as feasible, encourage conflicting views that do not get resolved, and expand rather than collapse the possibilities.

Given that learning is self-organizing,[21] perhaps curriculum can better be viewed as self-organizing. This reverses Ramus' idea. Instead of finding a structure of knowledge and assuming that learning should accommodate that structure, we are suggesting that curriculum should be designed to reflect the way people learn.

William Doll's Curriculum as Matrix

William Doll sees curriculum as process rather than content, as generated rather than predefined, as indeterminate rather than bounded, and as exploring the "fascinating imaginative realm born of God's laughter."[22] Doll believes that the heart of curriculum is a self-organizing, transformative process of negotiated passages between self, other, text, environment, and culture. This is a radical move, transforming the learner from spectator to co-constructor of knowledge. It is a move necessitated by our new understanding of the self-organizing nature of learning. Doll has organized his idea about curriculum as a matrix of four Rs: richness, recursion, relations, and rigor.[23]

Richness

By richness, Doll refers to a curriculum's depth, its layers of meaning, and its multiple possibilities or interpretations. He proposes that a rich curriculum will have "the 'right amount' of interdeterminacy, anomaly, inefficiency, chaos, disequilibrium, dissipation, lived experience." The right amount cannot be determined ahead of time. It is negotiated, Doll says, between students, teachers, and texts. Such a curriculum, Doll says, will be "provocatively generative without losing form or shape."[24]

Academic disciplines have their own form or shape that must be honored or we abandon our primary mission as a college, university, or divinity school. Each of us must examine the nature of our discipline and come to an understanding of its structure, its "historical contexts, fundamental concepts, and final vocabularies."[25] This is as far as some of us have gotten in constructing curriculum. It is necessary, but not sufficient, to consider the discipline *in itself*. We must also consider the discipline in the context of *these people*. We have to consider who our students are, what they will be doing, and what this class can contribute to their lives. When students graduate with a bachelor's, master's, or doctoral degree, it is common to welcome them to the company of educated women and men. The meaning of that phrase is not clearly established and, we contend, not static or fixed. What it means to be an educated woman and man today is not the same as what it meant a decade ago or what it will mean a decade hence.

It is difficult for many of us to abandon what Lyotard calls the grand narrative. Recovery of the richness that allows self-organization and transformation means that we abandon hope of bringing students to some coherent, consistent, right, or best understanding. But, as Doll observes, indeterminate is not arbitrary. Post-modern curriculum does not ask us to abandon theory, but rather to expand curricular space so that there is room for more than one perspective and for the messy sort of knowledge that is generated when theory is contextualized in real life experience.[26] Richness is not something we have to create. Classes are, by their nature, rich. We have to find ways to remove barriers to this richness.

Another condition for the expression of richness is to create spaces where diversity of views is honored and encouraged. Students who can express ideas without danger of being wrong, being criticized, or dismissed are more likely to bring minority views into the discourse. In 1892, Anna Julia Cooper (a voice from the

South) said:

> It is not the intelligent woman vs. the ignorant woman, nor the white woman vs. the black, the brown, and the red—it is not even the cause of woman vs. man. Nay, 'tis woman's strongest vindication for speaking that the world needs to hear her voice. . . . The world has had to limp along with the wobbling gait and the one-sided hesitancy of a man with one eye. Suddenly the bandage is removed from the other eye and the whole body is filled with light. It sees a circle where before it saw a segment. The darkened eye restored, every member rejoices with it.[27]

Welcoming diversity in thought and life history does not mean that we create an environment based on opinion, that all ideas are equal or that we will not disagree, sometimes passionately. It means that we value students' thinking, we honor where they are in their growth, and we are committed to learning together.

Susan Simonaitis expresses well the tensions that can arise from the creation of rich spaces for teaching as conversation. Quoting from Sharon D. Welch's *Sweet Dreams in America: Making Ethics and Spirituality Work,* Simonaitis supports Welch's belief that we need both "an ethic of conflict" and an "ethic of care" in the classroom:

> . . .it is crucial to know that . . . this class is not a safe place. We are discussing volatile issues and there will be areas of profound disagreement. We enter this discussion as individuals and as groups with radically different histories and experiences. . . . There are power differentials between us. . . . In trying to learn from each other, to learn how to work together, it is essential that we acknowledge that this is painful, difficult, and possibly exhilarating work. We do not know if we can trust each other. . . . [W]e are *likely* to offend, disappoint, and surprise each other, and we will probably be hurt and challenged. We are not, therefore, in a safe space. However, we are in a space for learning, a space in which we may learn how to work with conflict and how to learn from each other.[28]

Recursion

Recursive processes are those that loop back upon themselves, a feature known as self-referencing. One of us (SR) first encountered the idea of recursion when she studied artificial intelligence. The other (TC) first encountered the idea of recursion when she studied compositional analysis and literary/rhetorical criticism of the Bible. Douglas Hofstadter observes that recursion characterizes Escher's art, Bach's music, Godel's mathematical theory, and some literature.[29] Artificial intelligence scholars simulated human thought processes by building computer programs with recursive procedures that use themselves in their own definition. Winston and Horn describe this "nesting of procedures, where one calls upon others to do part of the work, like people do when working in a mature bureaucracy. Here, however, the procedure calls upon *itself,* either directly or through an intermediary, to tackle a subtask. This is called *recursion.*"[30]

Recursion is another condition necessary for a complex system to become self-organizing and, thus, transformative. Doll speaks of the "human capacity of having thoughts loop back on themselves. Such looping, thoughts on thoughts, distinguishes human consciousness; it is the way we make meaning."[31] Daniel Siegel says that "the development of mind has been described as having 'recursive features.' That is, what an individual's mind presents to the world can reinforce the very things that are presented."[32]

Recursive curriculum, according to Doll, has "no *fixed* beginning or ending. As Dewey has pointed out, every beginning emerges from a prior ending."[33] What we choose as a beginning is not *the* beginning but, as Gregory Bateson says, a point at which we have chosen to punctuate it.[34] Doll proposes that in a recursive curriculum every event is seen as an opportunity for reflection. It is not only the end in the sense of the completion of a project, but also the "beginning of another—to explore, discuss, inquire into both ourselves as meaning makers and into the text in question."[35] Curriculum is not a linear progression from beginning to end, neither does it thrive from repetition.

Recognizing the recursive nature of thought and designing recursive curriculum implies that we will expect loops in the content. We may revisit earlier concepts. Students may appear to regress or go on tangents when, in fact, they may be re-conceptualizing ideas. Assignments become points in a process rather than end products. Doll says, "Dialogue becomes the sine qua non of recursion: without reflection—engendered by dialogue—recursion becomes shallow not transformative; it is not reflective recursion, it is only repetition."[36] Recursive curriculum also means that we do not treat a topic and then move on. In our early years we were trying to be efficient about curriculum and to teach ideas in some logical sequence. What we try to do now is to tolerate redundancy in the curriculum, and to bring ideas forward as we move through the semester. Some students make sense of cognition, for example, when we are studying how students think about identity or moral development, rather than when we are studying cognition.

Relations

Doll describes two types of relations in curriculum: pedagogical and cultural.[37] Pedagogical relations are those within the curriculum, and cultural relations are those that interconnect ourselves, local culture, global, and even ecosystem and cosmology.

Pedagogical relations, Doll says, give curriculum depth. Such relations acknowledge that development is always occurring, that conditions, situations, and relations are always changing; the curriculum frame at the end is not the same as at the beginning. Doll says that relations are treated as contingent, hopeful that they will be "positively and communally developed."[38] The syllabus, which used to be the contract between us and the student, for example, has become an opportunity for us to share with students our views of the contribution this class might make and the general way we might go about things. Where we used to specify exactly what the assignments will be, we now state in a general way how we think we will proceed. Where we used to include a calendar of topics and assignments, we now list a general probable order of topics. We try to convey in the syllabus a looseness bound only by the constraint that keeps the class from losing its identity.

Doll says that his syllabus lists common readings for only two-thirds of the course. For the last one-third, the various groups choose from a selected list. We sometimes ask students to read common readings, and sometimes we ask them to read different texts on the same topic. For example, we might ask students to read all of the texts for the class, but they can read them in any order they choose. In class discussions there is a richness that comes from the students' readings that we do not find when everyone reads the same text at the same time. The discussion seems to focus more on connections. Doll says that he uses class time to interconnect the readings to the common readings and to each other. Because of the nature of what and who we teach, we also use class time to build bridges between text and experience, between text and tacit knowledge, the knowledge carried in experience.

Doll uses the term cultural relations, to refer to the matrix in which curriculum is embedded. Cultural relations extend beyond ourselves, Doll says, to include even the ecosystem and the cosmos. Cultural relations might also include what Gregory Bateson calls "deutero-learning."[39] He says that when studying a scientific idea, such as photosynthesis for example, we learn not only about photosynthesis, but also about the nature of science, about learning, and about other ideas that are generally an unrecognized and unplanned part of a class.

When we view people as a system, we look at the relations and interactions; we see the connectedness. In the language of chapter three,[40] we see them more like the river delta than a machine. In terms of curriculum, this has meant that, as part of the system, we can contribute to change in the system by changing what we are doing rather than trying to change the students. Like the river delta, we cannot predict what will change, but because we are interconnected and interacting, something will change. It has been our experience that the most difficult moments in teaching are those when we are stuck—iterating through an endless loop or immobilized. In those cases a change of some sort is helpful, as long as the change does not diminish the conditions necessary for a complex system to self-organize.

The nature of a class as a complex system has also led us to pay attention to resistance. In our early teaching we attributed resistance to attitude, assuming that there was something wrong with the students. Now we assume that we can learn from the resistance. Fleener describes a study that, instead of assuming that the failure of females in mathematics was due to a deficient math gene, asked why women found mathematics so inhospitable. She suspects that it is because women reject the underlying logic of domination.[41]

Our response to resistance in our early teaching was to fault the students. That, of course, only made their resistance worse. When we began to pay attention to the resistance, to befriend it and try to understand it, we found that it could teach us.

Rigor

Doll's fourth R, Rigor, is one that is used on our campus as a sledgehammer, often with a tone of superiority, by professors complaining about grade inflation and saying that they are rigorous because they give very few As. Doll redefines rigor as "purposely looking for different alternatives, relations, connections," a "conscious attempt to ferret out these assumptions, ones we or others hold dear, as well as negotiating passages between these assumptions, so the dialogue may be meaningful and transformative."[42]

Curriculum as Autobiography

Early in 1976, curriculum scholars William Pinar and Madeleine Grumet published a text, *Toward a Poor Curriculum,* that has now become a classic in exploring learning as "synthetical moments" and autobiography as an act of resistance.[43] This work and later books by Pinar, as well as the works of other curriculum scholars, led to a reconceptualization of the field of curriculum theory, now called curriculum studies to distinguish it from the pre-1970s ideas of curriculum. The movement to change the field of curriculum studies "emphasized the significance of subjectivity to teacher, to study, to the process of education."[44]

A central feature of this reconceptualization, according to curriculum studies scholar Patrick Slattery, is its attention to autobiographical and phenomenological experience. Slattery illustrates the use of autobiography in the following reflection from his own childhood: "As a child I often visited my grandmother's home in Shreveport, Louisiana. There was an unusual tradition in the family that had been passed down to each new generation. The children would gather around to listen to stories about the Civil War while my grandmother would rub the side of her head and say 'The damn Yankees shot Aunt Dora!'"[45] After recounting the rest of the story, he then added, "I do not remember studying the Civil War in any detail in elementary school, high school, or college, even though my transcripts indicate that I have credit for several courses in American history. Not once do I remember studying anything about the siege of Vicksburg[46] and, unfortunately, no teacher ever encouraged me to share my family tradition."[47]

Pinar calls for curriculum as complicated conversation. He argues for curriculum as scholarly discourse situated in human culture. He further characterizes academic discourse as living traditions that are, according to Arthur Applebee, "dynamic and changing, learned through participation, and focused on the 'present and future rather than the past.'"[48] Pinar calls for curricular experimentation according to student concerns and faculty interest and expertise.

Relationships in a Complex System

For much of our early teaching careers, we assumed that teaching caused learning. That is, we assumed that we were responsible for what students learned and that what we did could cause a change in students. Then one day, one of us (SR) read about structural coupling, a term invented by Humberto R. Maturana and Francisco J. Varela to describe the fact that in social interactions what appears causal is often only historical. They helped us to understand that what we do affects students, but rather than causing learning, the most we can do is to trigger learning. The way in which this triggering occurs most often is either through a perturbation in the environment (including, but not limited to us) or by the need to coordinate actions (for example, to solve a problem).

Doll says "as teachers we cannot, do not, transmit information directly; rather, we perform the teaching act when we help others negotiate passages between their constructs and ours, between ours and others. This is why Dewey says teaching is an interactive process with learning a *by-product* of that interaction."[49]

Structural coupling as a way of thinking about teaching says, among other things, that we are not responsible for the students' learning. We cannot plan a class around what students need to know. We can only plan for what we are able to provide. This does not mean that we ignore student needs and blame them if they don't get it. What students are doing and thinking matters. When we design classes what we really have is a tentative plan that will be embedded in feedback loops so that it can self-correct over time. If we hold our plans lightly there is a good chance that the students will use them for their benefit or we will see how something else might benefit them more, but it is *their* learning.

Who Are Our Students?

As we think about curriculum, we think first about our students. We try to imagine what it is like to come from their many backgrounds and histories. We imagine what it is like to be undergraduate students with so many questions and possibilities and a heady new sense of freedom. We think about graduate students with rich life experiences and professional goals. What all students have in common is that in some way college or graduate school is a time of expansion or possible expansion of experiences and ideas. As Perry says, "A fundamental belief in students is more important than anything else. This fundamental belief is not a sentimental matter: it is a very demanding matter of realistically conceiving the student where he or she is, and at the same time never losing sight of where he or she can be." Perry sees students as "courageous human beings who needed company and understanding along the way."[50]

Perry describes undergraduates, in part, as moving from "silence into agency and voice."[51] One of us (SR) experienced this in a powerful way one year when teaching an honors seminar in values. Since she is not an ethicist, Sherrie changed the topic to valuing, which had more of a psychological dimension for her. The class was a seminar made up of a small number of students. Sherrie divided the class into three parts, each of which required a paper or papers. Part one was an exploration of ourselves as *caring* people. Using Nel Noddings' book *Caring*,[52] she generated questions that the students answered in brief papers, after which they wrote a paper on themselves as caring people. She enjoyed watching as students moved from believing that they were apathetic to discovering how deeply they cared about social issues and how powerless they felt to address these issues. In the second part of the class, each student researched an issue they cared about, designed some action to make a difference, and carried out their plan. They all helped each other, and as part of their plan, they evaluated its impact. The last paper was a reflection again on themselves as caring people. It was powerful for Sherrie to see these students come to life and sense how their talents and skills could be used to address real problems about which they cared. It was moving to hear them say things like "my major taught me what I want to do, but this class has taught me who I want to be."

Perry says that Henry Adams made the following remark about his classmates in the 1850s: "the students had nothing to give each other because they had been 'brought up together under like conditions.'"[53] Our students have moved into a world of people whose homes are different from theirs, whose families, assumptions, beliefs, and ways of making sense of the world are very different from theirs. Any of us in a committed relationship that includes living together can remember how many of our assumptions, even about little things, became visible as we encountered someone whose assumptions were different. While college is not marriage, it is a step into a world of people unlike those we have known or imagined. This is such an important part of the university experience that if our classes are not diverse, we bring in diverse points of view and experiences. In some classes, the diversity is so rich that we have only to create the conditions to honor the perspectives in the class so that they will be brought forward.

The need for diversity grows more urgent as the world becomes more interdependent and complex. Perry says that "the increased mobility of the population at large, together with the new mass media, make the impact of pluralism part of the experience in the society as a whole. The growing person's response to pluralism in thought and values, and indeed his capacity to generate pluralism himself, are therefore critical to the destiny of a democracy."[54] Similarly, Sharon Daloz Parks proposes that "democratic societies are dependent upon a complex moral conscience— a citizenry who can recognize and assess the claims of multiple perspectives and are steeped in critical, systemic, and compassionate habits of mind."[55]

The question "who are our students" is not only about the particular people who will be in our classes, but also about who undergraduate and graduate students are, generally. We were talking with some colleagues about students. One of the professors was bemoaning the fact that students were not prepared for class discussion. He talked about how he threatened them and bawled them out. Earlier he had talked about what he wrote in his syllabus to warn them about his class. We have all done similar things. Today we see it differently. We want to help students overcome those deficiencies. If students do not know how to think about relationships, then we create assignments and experiences that will help them learn how to do that. If they do not know how to use resources to write a paper, we teach them how. Requiring more or trying to coerce them is doomed to fail. Coercion champions our own authority; it does not foster caring environments and communities in which we trigger learning. Curriculum needs more playfulness, more indeterminacy, and greater attention to how students learn through self-organization.

CHAPTER SIX

Changing Ideas about Communities of Learning

This medieval octagonal design with bastions seems to have existed only on the floor of the cathedral in Reims, France. **Courtesy Jeff Saward, photographer.**

"Because life in a complex and changing society is confusing, the temptation is to stand still and wait for things to clear up, to wash out, to become right again. But that is not patience; that is indifference."

Joan Chittister (*Becoming Fully Human,* 80)

Caring Relationships

In healthy families adults assume a teaching role within the context of the family relationships, making these adults the first and arguably the most important teachers that the child experiences. Certainly, a child learns a great deal in a relatively brief period of time. This relationship is rooted in what Nel Noddings argues is the fundamental ontological relationship, in which "we recognize that human encounter and affective response is a basic fact of human existence."[1] Max van Manen similarly argues for the relationship, which he calls pedagogical thoughtfulness, a fundamental teaching relationship. He says, "The child is in a real sense the agent of his or her own destiny—at both the individual and the social level. So a new pedagogy of the theory and practice of living with children must know how to stand in a relationship of thoughtfulness and openness to children and young people."[2] This fundamental pedagogical relationship is the historical root of teaching.

Noddings describes a caring teacher as follows:

Suppose, for example, that I am a teacher who loves mathematics. I encounter a student who is doing poorly, and I decide to have a talk with him. He tells me that he hates mathematics. *Aha,* I think. *Here is the problem. I must help this poor boy to love mathematics, and then he will do better at it.* What am I doing when I proceed in this way? I am not trying to grasp the reality of the other as a possibility for myself. I have not even asked: *How would it feel to hate mathematics?* Instead, I project my own reality onto my student and say, *You will be just fine if only you learn to love mathematics.* And I have 'data' to support me. There is evidence that intrinsic motivation is associated with higher achievement . . . so my student becomes an object of study and manipulation for me. . . . Bringing him to love mathematics is seen as a noble aim. And so it is, if it is held out to him as a possibility that he glimpses by observing me and others; but then I shall not be disappointed in him, or in myself, if he remains indifferent to mathematics. It is a possibility that may not be actualized. What matters to me, if I care, is that he find some reason, acceptable in his inner self, for learning the mathematics required of him or that he reject it boldly and honestly. How would it feel to hate mathematics? What reasons could

I find for learning it? When I think this way, I refuse to cast about for rewards that might pull him along. He must find his rewards. I do not begin with dazzling performances designed to intrigue him or to change his attitude. I begin, as nearly as I can, with the view from his eyes: Mathematics is bleak, jumbled, scary, boring, boring, boring. . . . What in the world could induce me to engage in it? From that point on, we struggle together with it.[3]

One element of caring, according to Noddings, is engrossment, a feeling with "the other." "I do not 'put myself in the other's shoes,' so to speak, by analyzing his reality as objective data and then asking, 'How would I feel in such a situation?' On the contrary, I set aside my temptation to analyze and to plan, I do not project; I receive the other into myself, and I see and feel with the other, I become a duality."[4] This kind of engrossment is a description of what it means to care for people and to care for ideas.

Teaching is a particular kind of engrossment in which we not only seek to understand the person as an autopoetic entity, but we also try to simultaneously understand the knowledge to which the person is relating. That is, as a professor, one of us stands in relationship with both the student and psychology, and on a particular occasion, the student and a particular idea. It is this kind of dual sight that makes teaching a unique kind of relationship.

When I first studied counseling, I had to learn theories and techniques and then I had to learn to get beyond them so that I could be fully present to the other person. The more I was in the moment, aware of the client and my reaction to him or her, the more likely it was that I would know what to say and do.

Teaching is like that for me. I have to prepare and then I have to leave the preparation behind so that I can be fully present to the students. On my best days of teaching I can listen with a third ear—to hear what students say and what is under what they say and what they are not saying. I find that I cannot think about other things and be present to a person in that way. I am not always able to do this, of course. My biggest obstacles are fear, ego, and stress. When I am afraid I automatically mount defenses that separate me from others. It reminds me of the TV show *Star Trek: The Next Generation* when they would order, "Shields up!" in response to a threat.

I had a student once named Fred who already had a Ph.D. in a science field and was now pursuing a master's degree. Fred was a thorn in my side. When I gave students a list of books from which to choose a reading, he got very upset and was quite vocal about it. He did not see how it would be fair to read different books and still take an exam. I told him that the book was just a tool for him to think with and the exam was an essay about his thinking, thus it did not matter which book he read. Further, I told him that the students could bring any material they wanted to help them with the exam. Fred continued to complain loudly, and on the day of the exam he brought in three shopping bags of materials. He sat in a chair surrounded by his props, which, to my knowledge, he never consulted.

Fred would also come into my office frequently with a question. I got very frustrated trying to deal with him. The more frustrated I got, the more I withdrew, and the more I withdrew the more Fred annoyed me. I asked a colleague for help, and she suggested that the next time Fred came in I should write about my feelings as he was talking. I did that and discovered that what bothered me about Fred was that he came in with a question but actually had something else in mind. He was manipulative, and my initial reaction to him was "shields up." I decided to use Fred as an opportunity for growth. I could practice on Fred and see what I could learn. This allowed me to be more open to Fred, and by the end of the semester Fred was talking about what a great class this was. I was still not overly fond of Fred, but he did not annoy me, and I did not withdraw from him. I have learned that I cannot selectively withdraw. For me, it is "shields up" or "shields down." If I shut Fred out, I shut the class out. They may not be able to identify it, but they can feel it, and they react to it.

I try to address my own mistakes with the class as soon as possible. Early in my teaching if I did something ill-considered I would ignore it and hope the class didn't notice either. The most extreme example of that was a swimming class I taught years ago. It was a class of over forty students in a pool with a deck that was about three feet wide. The students lined up along the pool, and I stood on the diving board because I didn't think they could hear me if I stood on the opposite deck. I was very nervous. As I began to talk to them I swung my arms forward and I fell in the pool. I just went down to the bottom and sat there thinking, irrationally, that they would just go away. I came up for air and they were, of course, still there. They applauded. I got even more embarrassed and sank to the bottom again. I finally realized that they weren't going away, so I got out and pretended nothing had happened.

Today when I make a mistake, I address it. I try to think about what will make it right. Sometimes I have to apologize to the class, and sometimes I apologize to an individual. Addressing my wrongs has kept the mistake from compounding into an obstacle, and at times it has brought us into a more effective relationship. I want to be clear that it is still an academic relationship, not a personal one. The invitation is not to draw close to me but to draw close with me to these wonderful ideas and insights. When students leave my class, if I am successful, they will be thinking about the ideas, not about me.

Preparing Myself for Class

I (SR) was visiting with a young friend named Scott, who has an excellent singing voice. I had just listened to a tape of his choir performance in a competition and was chilled by the sound of those young voices blended to make such beautiful music. I asked him if he had ever studied piano or any instrument. He looked a bit stunned and replied, "My voice is my instrument." Teaching is much like that. I forgot, or perhaps never knew, that the professor is the instrument in higher education. I try to prepare well for my classes. In fact, I have sometimes over-prepared out of fear of being in there with nothing. What usually happened was that I prepared reams of materials and then, after getting in the class with the students (whose contribution I could not anticipate fully in my planning), I did not use the things I had prepared. Early in my teaching I would berate myself for getting off the subject or wasting time. Worse, sometimes I would use my materials and follow my plan with a sort of intense loyalty. The lectures on those days were much more logical, flowed smoothly from one well-defined concept to the next. The only problem was that usually by the end of the class I was the only one still following this tidy, neat presentation.

This had been an ongoing dilemma for me. I have two conflicting intuitions: I know that preparation is important and that I have to leave it behind when I get to the class. I see now that I was confused about what was being prepared. Instead of planning a class, what I must do in preparation for a class is to prepare myself. I read, think deeply, play with various ways of representing ideas and concepts. Since I am teaching subjects in which I am well educated, it is a matter of taking time to continue to keep abreast and to think about ways to communicate these ideas to others. I become a well-formed instrument.

Another thing I have found helpful is to block off time before class to go for a walk or get a cup of coffee, or read something interesting. This puts me in a frame of mind that is more suitable to the kind of class atmosphere I want to create. When I go to class, at that moment the nature of my task changes. It is not an extension of the preparation time in which I go to students and present to them the result of my thinking (the way I used to do it). It is a dynamic, real-time interaction with real people in which the others in the class are invited to embark on a journey with me. I may begin by showing them some things that I have seen, but it is their journey too, and as they begin to ask questions and respond to what we are doing, they sometimes see things I missed because their background and experiences are different from mine. Sometimes their comments lead us into new territory. Sometimes they just come along for the ride. One of the side benefits to this approach to preparation is that it is more fun for both students and me. It is boring for us to go over things when the fun part, the thinking, has already been done.

Another myth that I held as a new professor was that I could somehow find the best way of teaching a particular class. One semester I would plan experiences; the next semester I would include more small group discussion, or whatever, in a never-ending search for the magic formula. The problem is that each semester the majority of people in the room (the students) changed. There is much about students of a particular class that is alike, but there is much more about them that is different. No wonder things that worked one semester do not seem to work the next. No wonder toward the end of the semester I would say to my colleagues "Now I think I've really got a handle on how to teach this class next semester. I'm going to do X (whatever the best thing was at the moment)."

The problem is not my inability to think about how to represent the concepts in that class. The problem was the persistence of the notion that I could find some universal plan that would apply no matter who registered for the class. Once I realized that I was preparing myself, instead of the class, then I also asked myself what I needed to be effective, given that I am going into a somewhat unknown situation, at least in the sense that the people in the class will probably take us some place unexpected.

At a university the most important assets are the two-legged ones that walk out the door at night, because real education happens at the interface between people. Materials and experiences are the props provided for the use of the people in the explorations in which they engage. To expect them to carry the teaching is to expect musical notes on a page to carry the music.

Using Feedback

Last night I (SR) began class by sharing with my students that I did not think some of the things we were doing were working the way I had hoped, and I would like to change them. This would have been unimaginable in my early years of teaching. At that time I would have planned everything, written it in the syllabus, and would have stuck to it no matter what. I don't know why I thought it was important to continue to do something that was not working, or why I thought the students would think that was a good idea.

Now, I understand that even the rather minimal planning that I do may not work the way I hope. I treat ideas—mine and the students'—about how we should proceed as tentative. We will begin to move in that direction, be sensitive to feedback, and make other decisions down the road. This is the kind of model that has proven effective with other complex dynamic systems: create initial conditions, and then make use of feedback loops. One form of feedback that I use extensively in the first few weeks of class is the quick write. I learned about this from a colleague, and I have found it quite valuable. In the last few minutes of class I ask students to take out a sheet of paper and write how things are going for them. I tell them that they do not need to put their names on the paper unless they are raising a question or an issue they would like for me to address with them individually. These quick writes have been quite valuable. They have allowed me to make many a mid-course correction.

For a long time I thought the importance of the quick write was that it provided me with information. I have discovered that it has a more subtle effect as well. Students have told me that it carried a message to them that it matters to me how they see the class because I ask and because I address their concerns. I don't always change things they don't like, but I do tell them why I won't or can't.

I try to remember that teaching should be interesting and fun. It is one of the most rewarding things I do overall. It has also, on occasion, been one of the most frustrating and annoying things I have done. Ironically, those are often the times I have learned the most if I have been able to become open enough to do so. I find it helpful to approach teaching with the goal of improving rather than trying to get it right. I do the best I can, learn what I can, and move on. There was a time when I took it all so seriously that every student who did not learn occupied my thoughts for days and every student who had an attitude precipitated deep soul-searching. That was not helpful. Teaching is part of my life. It is not life. Overall, if I am open to change, awareness, and seeking help, my teaching improves and I enjoy it more and more. I don't think I can ask for any more than that.

When it works, teaching is wondrous. As Daniel Seigel says, "When interpersonal communication is 'fully engaged'—when the joining of minds is in full force—there is an overwhelming sense of immediacy, clarity, and authenticity."[5] Those are the days when I am glad to be a professor. I am still amazed and grateful that I get to spend part of my professional life in the sacred space that we call teaching and in the unique relationships that occur in that space. I hope we will guard it with vigilance.

Faculty and Community

Most of us ended up as faculty because at some point in our lives we fell in love with learning. Unfortunately, after we have been teaching for a while our love can begin to dim. One of the most important things we can do as professors is to remain alive to loving learning. The factory metaphor has not just affected the way universities think of students, it has infiltrated the entire university. Some professors have become so concerned about production that they have converted their intellectual life to a series of deadlines and performances. How can being dutiful sustain love of knowledge?

If I (SR) want to have fun with my teaching, I need a community of other faculty who also love teaching and are willing to talk about it with me. I am not thinking about workshops and techniques here. I am talking about the kind of gut-wrenchingly honest conversation that most of us are afraid to have because we are afraid we will not look good. When I can put my fear and ego aside, and approach another colleague who loves teaching as I do, I have found the exchange quite fruitful.

I am cautious about the persons with whom I share. I have to feel safe with them. For me, that means that they will not laugh at me or put me down. It also means that we can have a conversation of equals, not novice and expert. It has to be someone who really cares about students and sees them as individuals. We do not have to agree and, in fact, it would not be too helpful if we agreed on everything, but we have to be interested in and respectful of each other's point of view. I feel very fortunate that I have colleagues with whom I can discuss teaching and, because they meet the above criteria, I can do so openly, without fear. I have people I can talk with when I am baffled about something in a class or frustrated with a student or myself. They listen and they share their experience. Sometimes their perspective gives me a new way to think.

Searching for Excellence

New ways of thinking come into play in constructing a community of learning devoted to excellence. Together, we need to give attention to what helps and what hinders people who come together around a common interest. Enlarging our definition of community, excellence, and ways of thinking about learning requires a cooperative, non-competitive, non-threatening, non-homogeneous effort. Nothing short of justice requires transformative change in teaching and learning.

Distinguishing indifference and dysfunction from impatience for something better is a job for the long haul. We are called to press on individually and institutionally to find ways in which to better support community and learning. First level tinkering has not—nor is there any reason to suspect it ever will—accomplished excellence or love of learning. Our times, despite (or perhaps on account of) their uncertainties and diversity, have created an openness to kinds of learning that promise enlarged understandings of excellence, even as they require second level, deep transformative change(s). We have a chance to foreground that which has too long been background, to bring to the center those whom our culture articulates as marginalized, for one set of reasons or another.[6]

Education in general and most particularly, from my perspective (TC), theological education needs more than linear or incremental adjustments, even if such changes implement fine new information and fine new ideas. New teaching strategies and methods are not enough, unless they accompany ideological changes in understandings of power, gender, sexuality, and distributive practices of all sorts. We are called to a new vision of community, with hope enough to go around.

We need what chaos scientists call a phase shift in our understanding of excellence.[7] Those who teach need "to envision an entirely new foundation for teaching, a new relationship with students, a new way of understanding ourselves and what we do."[8] Sherrie characterizes the difference between surface changes and a deeper kind of change that alters the very foundation on which we stand this way: "If I am sleeping and having a nightmare, a first order change is the equivalent of changing dreams. A second order change is the equivalent of waking up."[9] As strongly attracted as we are to the importance of a dream to call us forward, in the case of educational excellence, waking up seems more the order of the day at both personal and institutional levels. Persistence and commitment matter too.

"The land of excellence," Robert Quinn cautions, "is safely guarded from unworthy intruders. At the gates stand two fearsome sentries—risk and learning. The keys to entrance are faith and courage."[10] Quinn argues that we wrongly seek "quantum leaps in our performance levels by pursuing a strategy of incremental investment."[11] He maintains rather that excellence is part of a dynamic process or cycle of "four distinct phases: initiation, uncertainty, transformation, and routinization."[12] He further adds that, "To remain healthy and vibrant, a system must continuously circulate through the transformational cycle."[13]

Quinn's diagram of the ongoing transformational cycle traces the beginning vision that initiates a desire to change and improve through the risk of implementation that it may be illusory or sound. Uncertainty is tested by intense, intuitive experimentation in which panic can follow if experiments with the vision continuously fail. On the other hand, if the experiments are confirmed or if the participants gain creative insight from failure, they enter the transformational phase in which the elements of a problem may be reframed or assembled in a new theory or new paradigm. Exhaustion threatens transformation as does stagnation that can result from the routinization of a new vision gone stale or past its time. "The change process will continue when there is an ongoing evaluation, reinvention, and realignment of self and the organization."[14] For Quinn, it is the willingness to risk persisting through fear and panic, disillusionment, exhaustion, and stagnation in articulating new visions of changing relationships that creates a climate for deep change.

Many of us recognize that there are imbalances, inconsistencies, and contradictions in what we believe about teaching and learning and what we do with our students. Piaget would say we are experiencing disequilibration.[15] We know that courage and commitment to a dynamic vision of maintaining connection to the past as well as commitment to a transformed future is a big order. Quinn's cautions about disillusionment, panic, exhaustion, and stagnation are real for teachers and for our students. I (TC), for example, want my students to learn both the content of the various theological disciplines and access the imagination to address the questions of their generation. If I dishearten or overwhelm them, they will never find the lens that best helps them see the connections called for by their times and their communities.

Even though we may want to wake up to a more excellent vision of community and education, many of the changes I (TC) see us making are more like changing dreams than they are like waking up. I continue tinkering with this and that in a course, even though I know change of a different order is needed. Sherrie tells me that we need a new story that will come from an "emergent order, not from control and authority, but as a result of the interdependence of the elements in it."[16] Such a story, I am beginning to grasp, is a gift of community.

A New Story

A new story began to take shape for me on an ordinary day when I (TC) was proctoring a mid-term examination for thirty-some master's level students in an introductory Hebrew Bible course. They were working steadily on an examination that covered the Pentateuch and Historical Books; I was reading M. Jayne Fleener's *Curriculum Dynamics: Recreating Heart* in preparation for a doctoral class on teaching and learning in higher education that Sherrie and I would teach later that week.

Fleener's book is "about envisioning a curriculum for postmodern (and post-postmodern times)."[17] I was captivated by her orientation: "Following a Wittgensteinian path, meaning is conveyed and transformed through language and our creative invention of ideas. Definitions of words can only be understood in the history and context of their use rather than an appeal to some underlying meaning or fixed reality. Meanings evolve as use and context change."[18] Glancing around the room at the students, I hoped they remembered what we had said on this topic, albeit from another perspective, when we read the Genesis creation stories where changing understandings of male and female and God illustrate her point.

In a section titled "Guiding Metaphors," Fleener's citation of Herbert Kliebard's (1998) delineation of the three metaphors that typically characterize approaches to curriculum design caught my attention:

> Production, growth, and journey metaphors pervade how we organize the curriculum and make sense of our goals for schooling. In particular, Kliebard suggests that these metaphors characterize distinct values for education, defining goals, and having implications for practice. According to Kliebard, these metaphors of education emphasize social efficiency, child study, and social reconstruction, respectively.[19]

Then Fleener's sentence that changed my day: "I have made it standard practice in many of my classes to ask students what their metaphors for schooling are."[20] I looked out at my students, busily writing their examinations, and wondered what their metaphors might be. I had never thought to ask them. What images come together to form their mental conceptions of schooling? I asked myself some critical questions: What is my metaphor for teaching? How have my metaphors changed across the years of teaching graduate theological education? What memories and hopes give shape to my metaphors? I have changed textbooks, assignments, types of assignments, and examinations, but has anything really changed?

I read further in Fleener that Jim Cummins and Dennis Sayers perceive that "differences in the purposes of schooling and organization of the curriculum often are only appearances and do not represent fundamental differences or underlying philosophies."[21] They suggest, for example, that the curriculum cycles and debates between content (traditional) focus and child-centered (progressive) approaches to the curriculum do not represent different approaches to curriculum inquiry but are merely different sides of the same coin reflecting Freire's famous 1970 banking metaphor.

> Education . . . becomes an art of depositing, in which the students are the depositories and the teacher is the depositor. Instead of communicating, the teacher issues communiqués and makes deposits which the students patiently receive, memorize, and repeat. This is the "banking" concept of education, in which the scope of action allowed to the students extends only as far as receiving, filing, and storing the deposits.[22]

Then, Fleener put words around the questions that had been taking shape in my heart for quite some time:

> Our ability to invent 'new' metaphors for schooling may be limited by our own modernist assumptions, paradigms, and underlying logic. How do we learn to see things anew, have different visions, or even know the different questions to ask? How can I help my students see education from a perspective that is not driven by modernist assumptions and methods? Is the banking metaphor so ingrained in our common experiences of commerce and commercialism that we, at least in the West, cannot but help collapse all attempts to re-vision schooling into a banking model?[23]

I looked out again at my students and thought about my metaphors for this introductory class across the years. I was stunned to realize how my metaphors cluster around growth and journey ideas that mask a banking concept of education. For example, I have sometimes thought of myself as welcoming students to the garden of my delights and dismay. What does that make me? What does it make the students? Am I simply a guide for tourists? Is the garden *mine* by virtue of my education?

I could see all too clearly how flawed my assumption was that since knowledge was life-changing for me, it would be the same for the students. The notion that I was going to share my wealth with them made my banking assumptions clear. And even worse, in the privacy of my own thoughts I have sometimes labeled students as green beans or chickadees—growth metaphors that suggest they are immature, and that my role is somehow to see to their development. No question about who gets to decide what we will learn in this scheme! While I regularly say that I want to form a community of learners, hierarchy grounds my metaphors. I seem to have breathed in a pyramidal order of transmission, even though I have known for a long time that teaching is not mechanical. I know that it is not a question of putting the pieces together properly that yields learning.

Fleener helped me to ask myself: what kind of community have I created and what kind of community do I want? I was flooded with additional questions. What about heterarchy with its web or network of interconnections? What does heterarchy mean for the classroom? Painfully, I saw myself as encrusted with modernist assumptions, despite my best efforts and interests.

On this day, I glimpsed the contours and impact of the characteristics of the new story Sherrie sees and that Schwartz and Ogilvy argue is emerging in every discipline. The new story is complex, heterarchical, holographic, indeterminate, mutually causal, morphogenic, and perspectival.[24]

My entry into this new story comes from my perspective and work in feminist criticism. I know that objectivity is hooey. Objectivity is a way in biblical studies of enfranchising some and disenfranchising others, of creating insiders and outsiders. Perspective, on the other hand, takes responsibility for its multiple positions, even as it faces its limitedness and incompleteness in the face of difference. That both male and female give flesh to the image of God in limited and incomplete ways is actually a very old story (Gen 1:27). In the academy and in our churches, objective definitions have too long given authority and weight to ideas about God and human beings that reflect what we have said the Bible says. More often than not, the Bible does not say what we have believed it says.

As a literary/rhetorical critic, I am good at looking at constituent parts. Form is constrained by the parts, but meaning—I have come to understand—is not determined or properly articulated by it. "The requirements for morphogenesis are diversity, openness, complexity, mutual causality, and indeterminacy."[25] There is nothing proper or particularly correct about any one reading. James Muilenburg's canon: "A proper articulation of form yields a proper articulation of meaning," once said it all for me. But now I want my students to know Muilenburg and more. Readings that carry meaning—multiple readings—are incorporated into complex feedback loops by those who are constructing meaning, or perhaps should we, with Mary Catherine Bateson, say "improvising" meaning?[26]

Things are not simple in theological education any longer. One privileged group of individuals (the objective ones are the one I know best!) no longer control or even know the entire discipline. Interdependence, not rugged individualism, is the model of our day. Linear, hierarchical maps of relationships fail to describe my field—or yours—with its rich and multiple complexities. Consequently, hierarchy is being displaced by emergent heterarchy. And mutual causality is replacing linearity.

All this came clear to me when I tried to describe Judith studies across the last hundred years for an article in *Currents in Biblical Research*.[27] By the 1980s, the field was changed—not changing—but changed. A relatively few authoritative readings were replaced by a proliferation of studies. Sorting these studies on Judith opened my eyes to the eclipse of ordered progression in biblical studies as a whole. Women, culturally diverse interpreters, and readings from plural social locations are in the field to stay. Biblical criticism simply is not what it used to be at the start of the twentieth century. Its trajectories have flown off into multiple different directions forcing us to redefine our interpretive circle. Females and males representing a broad spectrum of ecumenical, interfaith, secular perspectives, with a variety of epistemological and ideological concerns now share a circle-like figure. But the boundaries of this circle are irregular, rich, multiple, and open, as I see it.

Metaphors for Teaching

The fact that my (TC) teaching needs to change should be no big surprise. I want in the next years of my career to articulate new metaphors that will serve as a platform for my teaching and learning. I took my dissatisfaction about teaching as inviting students into the garden of my delight and dismay to our class on teaching and learning. Sherrie suggested I might think about meeting the students in the garden and letting each one get there on their own path instead of following me in. Something forever changed for me on that day. New perspectives are emerging from my disequilibrium that I don't want to miss. I cannot think of any greater delight than finding meaning in teaching that interprets my past and shapes my present and future! From Ezekiel, I know that I have to let go of the old city to inherit the new. I also know this is the story that ends exile. From students and colleagues I am learning that transformation itself is a process.

One of my colleagues, Daisy Machado, uses the metaphor of the borderland to tell the story of the neglected history of the Latina/o church in the United States and to open discussion of the experiences of those who are marginalized:

> Latinas/os are a borderland people who live continuously cross borders
> that are more difficult to navigate than the ones that can be identified on a
> map. Our crossings have to do with linguistic, cultural, racial, economic,
> and social borders. Being Latina/o in the U.S. is about both belonging and
> being rejected, about being born on U.S. soil yet remaining foreign. It is
> about ambivalence. As Gloria Anzaldúa has said: 'The ambivalence from
> the clash of voices results in mental and emotional states of perplexity.'[28]

Ambivalences about her disciples facilitate cognitive shifts and an emergent new story about teaching for her:

> Yet while I have used the term borderland for my analysis of history and
> Latino/a identity, I have never really connected it to my teaching . . . until
> now. The more I think about it the more I see my classroom as a borderland.
> In the classroom both the students and I must cross borders if we are to
> connect and if learning is to happen.
>
> In the eleven years I have been teaching, 99.9% of my seminary
> students have been Euro-American and African American and I have just
> come to realize how many borders I have had to cross in order to connect
> with them. I have had to always speak English, which is not my first
> language. I have always had to know the history of their nation, since I
> am foreign born. I have had to try to understand their stories because they
> come from a context I am often at a loss to understand. And I have often
> found myself ambivalent about them, because I really do not understand
> them, and about myself because I know that they do not understand me.
> And as a result of navigating learning in this borderlands setting, in my
> years of teaching some class situations have been filled with both laughter

and tears. Sometimes the tears have been mine. Sometimes my students have shed them, and I have come to realize that they too have been crossing borders in order to understand and hear me.

Some students will cross only so much and will stop, thinking the effort is not worth it. Others, more daring and willing to go beyond their comfort zones, have made the effort to meet me, to truly listen to me, and some have become friends. Border crossing, of any kind, requires risk taking.

The same holds true for the classroom. My students and I are risk takers and in that process become vulnerable and in our vulnerability we are able to listen and to learn and to create—new ideas, new knowledge, and new hopes. We are able to see the fluidity of the ideas exchanged in the classroom to fuel our own theological formation and transformation. In the borderlands classroom all of us embark on a journey and how far we travel is only limited by our reluctance to cross borders.[29]

It is energizing and interesting to me when I hear the new stories that we tell together.

Seeing and More

Toni asked us today what metaphor we would use to describe teaching. While no verbal metaphor can capture the complex image I (SR) have in my head or the intuitive sense of teaching that I refer to in the still, quiet place inside, it was a fun discussion. The closest I could come is that there are many paths coming into a main path on which the students and I are walking. We have come from many places and bring some part of the place, the people, and our own intellectual and experiential history with us. We walk together on the path for a while. We also share the path with the invisible presence of our intellectual ancestors in the discipline. We do not walk as equals. I have walked the path for many years and have had the company of the ideas and theories of my discipline. The students are here for the first time. We walk in companionship the way I have often walked with young friends. We share the time and the path, and I share with them what I know about it from my experience. They share with me what they see from their unique perspectives. Together we see something new. It is like the stereopticon I looked through as a child. There was an image on the left and an image on the right that I looked through with the left and right eye, but the image I saw wasn't in the image seen by either eye. It emerged from the interaction of those images.

Caring about Students

M. Jayne Fleener says, "My teaching radically changed when I stopped thinking of students, learning, knowledge, teaching, and schooling as 'things' from a production perspective. Even ecological or growth metaphors didn't really work for me until I started thinking of students, learning, and schooling as *relationships and contextual.*"[30] A few years ago people began to talk about university students as "customers." I (SR) guess that is better than talking about them as "products" (which I have also heard), but I objected to it. When I expressed that objection, someone said, "Well, then, what would you call them?" I said "students." The professor-student relationship is a unique relationship with its own characteristics, unlike any other relationship.

I was a first–generation college student and from a different background than the other students I met. I stayed in college because I fell in love with learning in the first semester I was there. One of the things I remember from that semester was sitting in class and listening to a professor who had such passion for what he was teaching that I got caught up in it. I remember thinking that he seemed to see something wonderful, something just beyond what I could see. Over time I learned to see through his eyes and his heart and then, finally, to develop my own.

It wasn't just that he cared about what he saw. He seemed to care very much that I see it too. In a personal communication to me, Nel Noddings once said that she had asked a number of people over the years to describe their best teacher. She said that no one ever talked about teaching methods, but they almost always mentioned how much the teacher cared about them and their learning. In my class on group dynamics I learned that the first question that has to be answered for group members before they can accomplish a task effectively is "Do I belong? Am I OK?" These appear to be deep human needs.

I (SR) did not understand this in the early years of my teaching. I did not even question the fact that I was the only one talking. I did not see that students needed to establish relationships with each other and with me. I did not understand the need to reassure students or to create an atmosphere of acceptance. Surely most of you are not that extreme, but I caution you that over time I have found more subtle forms of these beliefs cropping up. At the other extreme, I have heard of professors who are so personal with their classes that the class content appears to be mostly about the professors and their emotional life. That is clearly not appropriate in my view.

The student as product metaphor assumes that teaching *causes* learning. Complex systems engaged in social life interactions are structurally coupled, not causal.[31] Such interactions also occur in classes with other learners, with a professor, with people who are present in the room through memory, books, movies, tape recordings, and one's own social and intellectual history. The complexity of these relationships is the source of its richness. We have not done a very good job of thinking about how to use the richness and complexity of these kinds of interactions to enlarge our understandings of community and to advance learning.

Relationality in Process

In searching for an image that brings together in a complementary way science (in terms of the quantitative) and story or narrative (in terms of the qualitative), William Doll makes a case for the figure of an open heart in which there is room for both and more. "In the space produced by feedback loops, the dance, or the play—this space of the 'third'—there exists, we believe 'spirit.' And it is spirit which education needs and sorely lacks. For in spirit, there exists—in all its awesome mystery—a vitality and in that vitality resides creativity."[32] Doll seeks a balance "that honors, utilizes the ineffable, the aesthetic, the creative, the passionate, the awe-inspiring." Science (logic/reason), story (culture/person), and spirit (life/breath/vital integrity)—three Ss—bring together a dynamic interplay of *passion and play* in his way of thinking.[33]

> My focus on this sense of a principal activating, animating, giving life to, endowing a situation with 'moreness' (to utilize Dwayne Huebner's word; 1999, pp. 403-404), is my belief, following Whitehead, that such infusing is necessary for 'keeping knowledge alive.' Such a process, active in nature, is itself a process. That is, any situation (and here I focus on teaching situations) can be more than it is by infusing that situation (experience, event, occasion) with spirit, or by finding the spirit that may well lie dormant within the situation. Whitehead, with his sense of the spiritful and spiritual—'the essence of education is that it be religious' (*Aims*, p. 14).— believes we need to find the 'relational essence' (*Science*, p. 88) of a situation. Relational essence focuses on a situation not being reified, not being a 'thing' isolated in itself (as so many school subjects are) but always in relation to the situation present.[34]

"Relationality itself as always being in process"[35] is the essence of what we have tried to address in this book. It is for us the recognition that Luke speaks of when the couple on the road to Emmaus meet Jesus "but their eyes were kept from recognizing him" (Luke 24:16) until they shared a meal. Jesus "took bread, blessed and broke it, and gave it to them. Then their eyes were opened, and they recognized him; and he vanished from their sight. They said to each other, 'Were not our hearts burning within us while he was talking to us on the road, while he was opening the scriptures to us?'" (Luke 24:30-32).

Open-hearted teaching/learning, we believe, is a relational, dynamic image that provides our complex, changing classrooms and institutions with a touchstone for new ways of thinking together about caring, community, and relationships with students and colleagues. We have shared with you our best understanding of change, higher education, and its geography. We hope that together with us you will discover an emergent new story, suitable and sufficient for our times. Feedback shapes its contours. Dialogue fosters its maturity and self-correction. It is a story about teaching and learning with room for passion, discipline, playfulness, transcendence, reverence, delight, and more.

Notes

Introduction

1. On the rich history of the labyrinth, see Saward, *Ancient Labyrinths of the World* and *Magical Paths*. All the labyrinths reproduced in this book are found at Jeff and Kimberly Saward's Web site "Labyrinthos" and are used with permission.

2. Artress, *Walking a Sacred Path,* xi.

3. Grace Cathedral's Web site features an "Online Finger Meditation Tool" that you may wish to explore.

4. Jim Day, personal communication.

5. *Tanakh* (or *Tenakh*) are Jewish names for this literature, also referred to as *Mikra* and *Holy Scripture(s)*. Some Christian Bibles include additional Old Testament books, known as the Apocryphal/Deuterocanonical Books.

6. Clarissa Pinkola Estés begins *The Faithful Gardener* with the epigraph: "New seed is faithful. It roots deepest in the places that are most empty." The book concludes with a prayer that counsels "no one can keep you from lifting your heart toward heaven—only you. It is in the middle of misery that so much becomes clear. The one who says nothing good came of this, is not yet listening" (76). A psychoanalyst interested in post-trauma work and the study of social and psychological patterns in culture, Estés is famous for her wisdom, commitment to justice, and 1992 book, *Women Who Run with the Wolves.* Her Guadalupe Foundation funds literary projects in this country, Madagascar, and Central America, providing local folktales and healthcare information that are used for learning to read and write.

7. In discussing "Old Testament" as a Christian convention and confessional term, Walter Brueggemann points out that as he uses the term he intends "to leave room and affirm that as Christians read this text toward the New Testament, so Jews properly and legitimately read the same scrolls toward the Talmud as the definitive document of Judaism." He deplores "Old Testament" as a term affirming "supersessionism (that is, that the New supersedes the Old and renders it obsolete)." See Brueggemann, *Introduction to the Old Testament,* 2.

8. Narrowly, *Mikra* "denotes the correct reading of the sacred words, as they have been handed down to us through the activities of numerous writers and copyists in the text of Tenakh," but in practice, the term *Mikra* is often used indiscriminately as a synonym for Hebrew Bible. See Mulder, *Mikra*, xxiii.

9. Our word "Bible" derives from Greek words, *ta biblia,* meaning literally "the books." Our habit of capitalizing this word in English gives the false impression that the books that comprise the Bible are more fixed than in fact they are. The Bible is not one collection under one cover.

10. Martin, "We are the Stories We Tell."

11. Daisy Machado, exploring the work of Martin Marty in "The Historical Imagination and Latina/o Rights," *Union Seminary Quarterly Review* 56 (2002):1-2.

12. A 2004 Wabash Center Mid-Career Grant funded these sessions. In addition, Toni Craven shared portions of this work with other participants in a Wabash funded Mid-Career Workshop (2002-2003).

13. Darren J. N. Middleton, Associate Professor of Religion, Texas Christian University e-mail message to authors, February 4, 2005.

14. Julius Tsai, Assistant Professor of Religion, Texas Christian University e-mail message to authors, February 10, 2004.

Chapter 1 Personal Change

1. Piaget, *Equilibration of Cognitive Structures.*

2. Norris, "Vocation in the Outback," 203.

3. Norris, *Dakota: A Spiritual Geography,* 63-64.

4. Ibid., 64.

Chapter 2 Emergent Change

1. Watzlowick, Weakland, and Fisch, *Change.*

2. In most instances from here on, we will use "we" or "one of us" (followed by the initials SR for Sherrie Reynolds or TC for Toni Craven) in place of "I" for ease of reading and because authorship is intermingled.

3. Fleener, *Curriculum Dynamics*, 116.

4. Joyce, "Julia and Mandelbrot Sets."

5. Ferns image: "Beaver Ferns," Outdoor Travels. Broccoli image: "Fractal Broccoli," Sullivan.

6. Williams, "Computing the Mandelbrot Set."

7. You can play the game at Voolich and Devaney, "The Chaos Game."

8. Following World War I, Waclaw Sierpinski (1882-1969) together with other mathematicians Kuratowski and Banach formed the "Polish School" to explore the then emerging field of abstract spaces. As early as 1915, Sierpinski described a "gasket" or a "triangle" with repeated and proportionally reduced areas, what we now recognize as "fractals." Given the recursive power of computers, Sierpinski's triangles have become some of the most recognizable shapes or patterns in all computer graphics. See Gray, Venit, and Abbott, "Sierpinski Triangles."

Chapter 3 Changing Ideas about Consciousness

1. Prigogine, *Out of Chaos*, xiii, and Alvin Toffler's influential trilogy: *Future Shock*, 1970; *The Third Wave*, 1980; *Powershift: Knowledge, Wealth, and Violence at the Edge of the 21st Century*, 1991.

2. Doll, *Post-Modern Perspective*, 59.

3. Fox and Sheldrake, *Physics of Angels*, 8-9.

4. Schwartz and Ogilvy, *Emergent Paradigm*, 2.

5. Ibid., v.

6. In *Theology for a Third Millennium*, Küng calls the forming paradigm of postmodernism a "megaparadigm" because of its epochal sweep.

7. Schwartz and Ogilvy, *Emergent Paradigm*, 15.

8. Ibid., 13.

9. Hayes and Holladay, *Biblical Exegesis*.

10. Ibid., 189.

11. See Stuart, "Exegesis," *Anchor Bible Dictionary* 2:682-688. His *Old Testament Exegesis: A Handbook for Students and Pastors* first appeared in 1980, with a second edition in 1984, and third edition in 2001.

12. Ibid., 682. Stuart's precision in knowing the right steps to follow and his conviction of their right order limits exegesis to the few qualified to do it (those who at a minimum could read the biblical languages, Hebrew and Greek). Consciousness of the right way to do exegesis was not consciousness of the consequences of this kind of thinking. It did little for the regular practice of exegesis, which became a remembered event, done once or twice in graduate school. Ironically, this way of thinking fostered a divide between how we do our own work and how we teach others. We may have taught that exegesis "places no premium on speculation or inventiveness," but publishing required just the opposite.

13. Ibid., 687.

14. Yee, *Judges & Method*.

15. Ibid., ix.

16. Ibid., ix.

17. See Segovia, *Toward Minority Biblical Criticism*; Patte, *Global Bible Commentary*; West, *Reading Other-Wise*.

18. Schwartz and Olgivy, *Emergent Paradigm*, 13.

19. For simulation and helpful online resources related to boids, see Reynolds, "Boids: Background and Update." Even though it is geese who fly in a v-shaped formation, our colloquial expression about having "ducks" in a row is popularly understood as described.

20. Taylor, *Luminous Web*, 57.

21. Ibid., 57.

22. Ibid., 58.

23. Ibid.

24. Ibid., 59.

25. Ibid.

26. Ibid., 60.

27. Dennis Gabor received the Nobel Prize in Physics in 1972 for his discovery of holography, which is "the only visual recording and playback process that can record our three-dimensional world in a two-dimensional recording medium and playback the original object or scene to the unaided eyes as a three dimensional image," "History of Holographic." See this site for overview and instruction in how to build and use a holographic recording system.

28. Bohm and Hiley, *Undivided Universe.*

29. Schwartz and Ogilvy, *Emergent Paradigm*, 54.

30. "Tenana River."

31. Gleick, *Chaos,* 15.

32. Ibid., 16.

33. Ibid., 23. To view the Lorenz Attractor, type into an internet search engine "Lorenz Attractor" for images and links.

34. See "Edward Lorenz." Lorenz did his graduate work at MIT and then spent his entire academic career there as first a staff member (1948-1955) of the Department of Meteorology and then as a faculty member (1956) and head of the department (1977 to 1981). He became an emeritus professor in 1987. In an autobiographical sketch, Lorenz said, "As a boy I was always interested in doing things with numbers, and was also fascinated by changes in the weather." While serving as a weather forecaster during World War II, his interest in why it is so hard to make good weather predictions led him to graduate school. His curiosity about mathematics and meteorology led to formulation of chaos theory, one of the most important changes in the twentieth century.

35. Gleick, *Chaos*, 23.

36. Ibid., 24.

37. Schwartz and Ogilvy, *Emergent Paradigm*, 56.

38. Wiener, *Cybernetics*, 2nd ed. adds a new preface and two supplementary chapters to what has been judged one of the seminal books of the twentieth century.

39. Rheingold, *Tools for Thought*, "Chapter Five Ex-Prodigies and Antiaircraft Guns" is available from MIT Press or online.

40. Bateson, *Our Own Metaphor*, 4-6.

41. Ibid., 5.

42. Papert, *Children's Machine*, 69.

43. Schwartz and Ogilvy, *Emergent Paradigm*, 14.

44. Extended discussion of the metaphysical split between body and soul appear in his *L'Homme* (1633), *Meditationes* (1641), and *Les passions de l'âme* (1649). Descartes is considered the father of both analytic geometry and modern rationalism. American functional psychology, the work of William James (1842-1910), and especially understandings of biological consciousness and the experience of the transcendent trace to the mind/body problem as posed originally by Descartes.

45. Schultz, *Modern Psychology*, 2nd ed., 19.

46. Wozniak, "Mind and Body."

47. Schwartz and Ogilvy, *Emergent Paradigm*, 53.

48. Ibid., 51.

49. Ibid., 52.

50. Whyte, *Unconscious Before Freud*.

51. Simon, *Jonah*, vi.

Chapter 4 Changing Ideas about Learning

1. The following is taken from David Balch's Brite Divinity School Annual Faculty Report, which he shared in an e-mail with the authors, March 2, 2004.

2. See *Higher Education Reconceived*, chap. 1, 7.

3. Holton, *Kepler to Einstein*, 371.

4. In 2005, Darwin's four great works (*Voyage of the HMS Beagle* [1845],
*On the Origins of Species by Means of Natural Selection, or the Preservation of
Favoured Races in the Struggle for Life* [1859], *The Descent of Man* [1871], and
The Expression of Emotions in Man and Animals [1872]) were published together
in *From So Simple a Beginning* with Edward O. Wilson's introductory essay for the
collection and an index for these classics. From this collection, see *Origins of
Species,* 371.

5. Bird, *Chaos and Life,* 29.

6. Darwin, "Introduction," xiv.

7. "People and Discoveries: Ivan Pavlov."

8. "Ivan Pavlov."

9. Ibid. Although Pavlov's experiments are commonly described as using a bell, he
actually used a number of auditory stimuli (metronome, whistles, air bubbling
through water) and "When, in the 1990s, it became easier for Western scientists to
visit Pavlov's laboratory in Moscow, no trace of a bell could be found."

10. Pavlov, "Conditioned Reflexes."

11. Cuny, *Ivan Pavlov,* 123.

12. "Watson's Childhood."

13. Schultz and Schultz, *Modern Psychology,* 8th ed., 175.

14. Ibid., 176.

15. "People and Discoveries: John Watson."

16. Vargas, "Biography of B. F. Skinner."

17. Ibid.

18. Ibid.

19. Ibid.

20. Schultz, *Modern Psychology,* 2nd ed., 246.

21. Skinner, "Operant Behavior."

22. Perry, *Intellectual and Ethical Development,* 65.

23. Hursh, Haas, and Moore, "Interdisciplinary Model," 37.

24. We also find the work of Parks, *Big Questions, Worthy Dreams,* xi, helpful in understanding learning. She has written about the "twenty-somethings" development as a "search for meaning, purpose, and faith." Formerly a professor at the Harvard Divinity School and the Weston Jesuit School of Theology, Parks has also held faculty and research position in leadership and ethics at the Harvard Business School and the Kennedy School of Government. Currently, she is associate director and faculty at Whidbey Institute.

25. Luria, *Making of Mind,* 19.

26. Engels, *Dialectics of Nature,* 291.

27. Vygotsky, *Mind in Society,* 20-26, 52-55, 132-133.

28. Riever, *Individual, Communication, and Society,* 21.

29. Ibid., 21.

30. Papert, *Children's Machine,* 69.

31. Piaget, *Equilibration of Cognitive Structures.*

32. Maturana and Varela, *Tree of Knowledge,* 119.

33. Maturana and Varela, *Autopoiesis and Cognition,* 78.

34. Harries-Jones, *Recursive Vision,* 68.

35. Ibid., 69.

36. Hawking, *Universe in a Nutshell,* 31.

37. Maturana and Varela, *Tree of Knowledge,* 137.

38. Eisner, *The Enlightened Eye,* 46.

39. Freedman and Combs, *Narrative Therapy,* 23.

40. Bateson, *Mind and Nature.*

41. Robert Romanyshyn, personal communication.

42. Feynman, *Surely You're Joking,* 157.

43. Ibid., 173.

44. Davis, Sumara, and Luce-Kapler, *Engaging Minds,* 19.

45. Quinn, *Deep Change,* 83.

Chapter 5 Changing Ideas about Curriculum

1. Doll, "Ghosts," in *Curriculum Visions*, 29. Doll suspects that the "course for running" is that run by chariots in the Circus Maximus racetrack. He tells a fascinating story of why Calvinist educational theory adopted the Latin word for racetrack to express its interest in a formalized course of school study, noting that in the sixteenth and seventeenth centuries "it was not common to think of life (or learning) as having the sort of sequential order that today we attribute to curriculum or curriculum vitae" (29). "Although the term *curriculum* appears nowhere in educational literature prior to Thomas Fregius's publication of Ramus's mapping of the structure of knowledge in 1576, it is true that John Calvin in his *Commentaries* (1540-1565) often refers to life as a 'race' or 'racecourse.' In fact, in his final (1559) edition of the *Institutes,* Calvin uses the phrases *vitae curriculum* and *vitae curriculo.* However, these phrases are used sparingly compared to the number of times he used *vitae cursu* or *vitae cursum*, alternative renderings for the 'course of life'" (29). Doll posits that *curriculum* as a "course-of-life" or method of study "provided the Calvinists, committed to a faith based on order and discipline, with a way to steer their youth through a world 'all in peeces,' one with 'all cohaerance gone' (Donne, 1968/1611), one clearly out of control" (33). Doll thus finds that "control as an operating concept is actually embedded in the history of curriculum from the very first usages of the word in an educational setting" (34). Doll concludes that "It is time to put this ghost to rest, to let it retire peacefully to the 'Land of No Return' and to liberate curriculum to live a sprightly life of its own" (34).

2. Foster, Dahill, Golermon, and Tolentino's *Educating Clergy* is the Carnegie Foundation for the Advancement of Teaching's first book in a series of comparative studies of professional education. The authors discuss the historic uniqueness in American theological education of Andover Theological Seminary: it was the first freestanding graduate school in the nation, it united traditional and strict Calvinists, and it organized its formal curriculum in Bible, doctrine, history, and homiletics (192-99). The ghosts (of control) that Doll describes are evident in Timothy Dwight's (1752-1817) vision for theological education as post-baccalaureate training, though he himself was a product of an apprenticeship model. Dwight's opening convocation speech at Andover in the spring of 1808 "proposed lofty educational standards for the institution that continue to influence assumptions about contemporary seminary education" (195). Emphasis persists in mainline Protestant seminaries on interpretation of classical texts (most importantly, the Bible) and performance or public oratory that shapes civic ideology (196-97).

3. Doll, "Ghosts," 31. The Ramist map: Doll, "Culture of Curriculum."

4. Doll, "Images of Curriculum," 79.

5. Doll, "Ghosts," 29.

6. Ibid., 40.

7. Ibid., 34

8. Ibid., 35.

9. Ibid.

10. Ibid., 42.

11. Ibid., 31.

12. Ibid., 33.

13. See chap. 4, "Changing Ideas about Leaning."

14. Fleener, *Curriculum Dynamics,* 43. See our earlier discussion of "Change as Fractal" and Fleener's "geometry of relationship" in chap. 2, "Emergent Change."

15. Ibid., 45.

16. See our discussion in chap. 3, "Changing Ideas about Consciousness."

17. Cilliers, *Complexity and Postmodernism,* 3.

18. Ibid.

19. Ibid., xxiv.

20. Ibid., 114.

21. See chap. 4, "Changing Ideas About Learning."

22. Doll, *Post-Modern Perspective,* 176.

23. Ibid. 174-183.

24. Ibid. 176.

25. Ibid.

26. In *Educating Clergy,* Charles P. Foster et al. claim that there are four signature pedagogies (interpretation, formation, contextualization, and performance) that speak both to theological educators and to the larger community of educators in the professions and the liberal arts. The diverse practices in Jewish, Catholic, and Protestant theological education are part of what the authors call "pedagogical imagination" (39).

27. Lemert and Bhan, *Anna Julia Cooper,* 107.

28. Simonaitis, "Teaching as Conversation," 113.

29. Hofstadter, *Godel, Escher, Bach.*

30. Winston and Horn, *LISP,* 63.

31. Doll, *Post-Modern Perspective,* 177.

32. Siegel, *Developing Mind,* 19.

33. Doll, *Post-Modern Perspective,* 178.

34. Gregory Bateson, *Steps to an Ecology of Mind.*

35. Doll, *Post-Modern Perspective,* 178.

36. Ibid.

37. Ibid., 179-183.

38. Ibid., 179.

39. Bateson and Bateson, *Angels Fear: Towards an Epistemology of the Sacred,* 17.

40. See chap. 3, "Changing Ideas about Consciousness."

41. Fleener and Dupree, "Autobiosophy." In the abstract the authors explain, " "Autobiosophy is an approach to critical social inquiry evolving from Wittgenstein's notion of confession and Foucalt's perspective of technologies of the self."

42. Doll, *Post-Modern Perspective,* 183.

43. Pinar and Grumet, *Toward a Poor Curriculum* .

44. Pinar, *What Is Curriculum Theory,* 4.

45. Slattery, *Curriculum,* 50-51.

46. Vicksburg is where the shooting of Aunt Dora occurred.

47. Slattery, *Curriculum,* 62-63.

48. Pinar, *What Is Curriculum Theory,* 193.

49. Doll, *Post-Modern Perspective,* 180.

50. Perry, *Intellectual and Ethical Development,* xii.

51. Ibid., xix.

52. Noddings, *Caring.*

53. Perry, *Intellectual and Ethical Development,* 6.

54. Ibid.

55. Ibid., 10.

Chapter 6 Changing Ideas about Communities of Learning

1. Noddings, *Caring*, 4.

2. van Manen, *Tact of Teaching*, 3.

3. Noddings, *Caring*, 15.

4. Ibid., 30.

5. Siegel, *Developing Mind*, 337.

6. In the 1974 French original *The Practice of Everyday Life,* Michel de Certeau argues that "Marginality is today no longer limited to minority groups, but is rather massive and pervasive . . . . Marginality is becoming universal. A marginal group has now become a silent majority" (xvii).

7. See *Higher Education Reconceived*, chap. 1, 2.

8. See *Higher Education Reconceived,* chap. 2, 10.

9. Ibid.

10. Quinn, *Deep Change*, 165.

11. Ibid.

12. Ibid., 167. Note the diagram on 168.

13. Ibid., 168.

14. Ibid., 169.

15. *Higher Education Reconceived*, chap. 4, 35.

16. Private conversation about the changing story as it relates to emergent order. See *Higher Education Reconceived*, chap. 3, 18.

17. Fleener, *Curriculum Dynamics,* 11.

18. Ibid., 11-12.

19. Ibid., 14.

20. Ibid.

21. Ibid., 14-15.

22. Freire, *Pedagogy of the Oppressed*, 58.

23. Fleener, *Curriculum Dynamics*, 15.

24. See *Higher Education Reconceived*, chap. 3, 12.

25. Schwartz and Ogilvy, *Emergent Paradigm*, 14.

26. Mary Catherine Bateson, *Composing A Life*, talks about the concept of improvisation as a lens for thinking about life as an "improvisatory," adaptive art in which we recombine familiar materials in new ways. She likens us to jazz musicians whose activity "is at once individual and communal, performance that is both repetitive and innovative, each participant sometimes providing background support and sometimes flying free," 2-4.

27. Craven, "Book of Judith," 187-230.

28. Daisy Machado prepared the following "Metaphor for Teaching," for a Wabash Pre-Tenure Theological School Faculty Workshop, in Crawfordsville, IN (June 11, 2004).

29. Ibid.

30. Fleener, *Curriculum Dynamics,* 80.

31. Maturana and Varela, *Tree of Knowledge.*

32. Doll,"Modes of Thought," 8. The open heart figure is found on p. 2.

33. Ibid., 9.

34. Ibid.

35. Ibid.

List of Works Cited

Artress, Lauren. *Walking a Sacred Path: Rediscovering the Labyrinth as a Spiritual Tool*. New York: Riverhead Books, 1995.

Bateson, Gregory. *Mind and Nature: A Necessary Unity*. New York: Hampton Press, 2002.

———. *Steps to an Ecology of Mind*. New York: Ballentine, 1972.

Bateson, Gregory, and Mary Catherine Bateson. *Angels Fear: Towards an Epistemology of the Sacred*. New York: Bantam Doubleday, 1988.

Bateson, Mary Catherine. *Composing A Life*. New York: Atlantic Monthly Press, 1989.

———. *Our Own Metaphor: A Personal Account of a Conference on the Effects of Conscious Purpose on Human Adaptation*. Washington: Smithsonian Institution Press, 1991.

"Beaver Ferns," Outdoor Travels, http://outdoortravels.com/files/wv_snosho_34_beaver_ferns.jpg.

Bird, Richard J. *Chaos and Life: Complexity and Order in Evolution and Thought*. New York: Columbia University Press, 2003.

Bohm, David, and B. J. Hiley. *The Undivided Universe*. New York: Rutledge, 1993.

Brueggemann, Walter. *An Introduction to the Old Testament: The Canon and Christian Imagination*. Louisville, KY: Westminster John Knox, 2003.

Burke, James. *The Day the Universe Changed*. Boston: Back Bay Books, 1995.

Chittister, Joan. *Becoming Fully Human*. New York: Rowman & Littlefield Publishers, 2005.

Cilliers, Paul. *Complexity and Postmodernism*. UK: Routledge, 1998.

Craven, Toni. "The Book of Judith in the Context of Twentieth-Century Studies of the Apocryphal/Deuterocanonical Books." *Currents in Biblical Research* 1.2 (April 2003): 187-230.

Cuny, Hilaire. *Ivan Pavlov: The Man and His Theories*. New York: Paul S. Eriksson, 1965.

Darwin, Charles. "Introduction." *The Origin of Species,* edited by Julian Huxley. New York: Penguin, 1958.

———. *On the Origin of Species by Means of Natural Selection, or the Preservation of Favoured Races in the Struggle for Life.* From the collection *From So Simple a Beginning: Darwin's Four Great Books,* edited by Edward O. Wilson. New York: W. W. Norton, 2005.

Davis, Brent, Dennis J. Sumara, and Rebecca Luce-Kapler. *Engaging Minds: Learning and Teaching in a Complex World.* New Jersey: Lawrence Erlbaum Associates, 2000.

de Certeau, Michel. *The Practice of Everyday Life.* 1974. Reprint, Steven Rendall, trans. Berkeley: University of California Press, 1984.

Doll, William E., Jr. "Complexity and the Culture of Curriculum," Louisiana State University, http://www.lsu.edu/faculty/wdoll/Papers/HTML/complexity_culture.htm.

———. "Ghosts and the Curriculum," in *Curriculum Visions,* edited by William E. Doll, Jr., and Noel Gough. Studies in the Postmodern Theory of Education, vol. 151. New York: Peter Lang, 2002.

———. "Images of Curriculum," Louisiana State University, http://www.lsu.edu/faculty/wdoll/Papers/HTML/images_of_curriculum.htm.

———. "Modes of Thought." In *Proceedings of the 2003 Complexity Science and Educational Research Conference.* October 16-18, 2003; Edmonton, Alberta, Canada, 8.

———. *A Post-Modern Perspective on Curriculum.* New York: Teachers College Press, 1993.

"Edward Lorenz, Father of Chaos Theory and Butterfly Effect, Dies at 90," *MIT News,* April 16, 2008, http://web.mit.edu/newsoffice/2008/obit-lorenz-0416.html.

Eisner, Elliott W. *Cognition and Curriculum Reconsidered.* 2nd ed. New York: Teachers College Press, 1994.

———. *The Enlightened Eye: Qualitative Inquiry and the Enhancement of Educational Practice.* New York: Prentice-Hall, 1997.

Engels, F. *Dialectics of Nature.* New York: International Publishers, 1968.

Estés, Clarissa Pinkola. *The Faithful Gardener: A Wise Tale About That Which Can Never Die.* San Francisco: Harper Collins, 1995.

———. *Women Who Run with the Wolves.* New York: Ballentine Books, 1992.

Pinar, William F. *What Is Curriculum Theory?* Mahwah, NJ: Lawrence Erlbaum Associates, 2004.

Feynman, Richard P. *Surely You're Joking, Mr. Feynman! Adventures of a Curious Character.* New York: W. W. Norton, 1985.

Fleener, M. Jayne. *Curriculum Dynamics: Recreating Heart.* Studies in the Post Modern Theory of Education, vol. 200, edited by Joe L. Kincheloe and Shirley R. Steinberg. New York: Peter Lang, 2002.

Fleener, M. Jayne, and Gloria Nan Dupree. "Autobiosophy through Gynocritical Inquiry: Exploring Women's Ideas about Mathematics, Power, and Community." *Journal of Curriculum Theorizing* (2002).

Foster, Charles R., Lisa E. Dahill, Lawrence A. Golermon, and Barbara Wang Tolentino. *Educating Clergy: Teaching Practices and Pastoral Imagination.* San Francisco: Jossey-Bass, 2006.

Fox, Matthew, and Rupert Sheldrake. *The Physics of Angels: Exploring the Realm Where Science and Spirit Meet.* San Francisco: Harper, 1996.

"Fractal Broccoli," Jon Sullivan, Free Public Domain Photo Database, http://pdphoto.org/PictureDetail.php?mat=pdef&pg=8232.

Freedman, Jill, and Gene Combs. *Narrative Therapy: The Social Construction of Preferred Realities.* New York: W. W. Norton, 1996.

Freire, Paulo. *Pedagogy of the Oppressed.* New York: Seabury Press, 2000.

Gleick, James. *Chaos: Making a New Science.* New York: Penguin Books, 1987.

Gray, Shirley B., Stewart Venit, and Ross Abbott. "Sierpinski Triangles," National Curve Bank, http://curvebank.calstatela.edu/sierpinski/sierpinski.htm.

Harries-Jones, Peter. *A Recursive Vision: Ecological Understanding and Gregory Bateson.* Toronto: University of Toronto Press, 1995.

Hawking, Stephen William. *The Universe in a Nutshell.* New York: Bantam, 2001.

Hayes, John H., and Carl R. Holladay. *Biblical Exegesis: A Beginner's Handbook.* 3rd ed. Louisville: Westminster John Knox, 2007.

"History of Holographic," Henglei Holographic, http://www.holographic.cn/History_of_hologram.html.

Hofstadter, Douglas. *Godel, Escher, Bach.* US: Basic Books, 1979.

Holton, Gerald. *Thematic Origin of Scientific Thought: Kepler to Einstein,* revised ed. Cambridge: Harvard University Press, 1988.

Hursh, Barbara, Paul Haas, and Michael Moore. "An Interdisciplinary Model to Implement General Education." *Journal of Higher Education* 54:1 (Jan-Feb 1983).

"Ivan Pavlov," Fact Index, http://www.fact-index.com/i/iv/ivan_pavlov.html.

Joyce, David E. "Julia and Mandelbrot Sets," Clark University, http://aleph0.clarku.edu/~djoyce/julia/julia.html.

Küng, Hans. *Theology for a Third Millennium: An Ecumenical View.* New York: Doubleday, 1988.

Lemert, Charles, and Esme Bhan, eds. *The Voice of Anna Julia Cooper, Including a Voice from the South and Other Important Essays, Papers, and Letters.* New York: Rowman & Littlefield, 1988.

Luria, Aleksandr R. *The Making of Mind: A Personal Account of Soviet Psychology.* Reprint ed. Cambridge: Harvard University Press, 1986.

Machado, Daisy. "The Historical Imagination and Latina/o Rights," *Union Seminary Quarterly Review* 56 (2002):1-2.

Martin, Wendy. "We Are the Stories We Tell." *New York Times Book Review,* Jan 8, 1988.

Maturana, Humberto R., and Francisco J. Varela. *Autopoiesis and Cognition: The Realization of the Living.* Boston Studies in the Philosophy of Science, vol. 42. Boston: Reidel, 1980. First edition published in 1973.

———. *The Tree of Knowledge: The Biological Roots of Human Understanding.* Boston: Shambhala, 1998.

Mulder, Martin Jan, ed. *Mikra: Text, Translation, Reading and Interpretation of the Hebrew Bible in Ancient Judaism and Early Christianity* (Compendia Rerum Iudaicarum ad Novum Testamentum). Asses/Maastricht; Van Gorcum and Minneapolis: Fortress, 1990.

Noddings, Nel. *Caring: A Feminine Approach to Ethics and Moral Education.* 2nd ed. with a new preface. Berkeley: University of California Press, 2003.

Norris, Frederick W. "Vocation in the Outback," in *The Scope of Our Art,* edited by L. Gregory Jones and Stephanie Paulsell. Grand Rapids: William B. Eerd mans Publishing Company, 2002.

Norris, Kathleen. *Dakota: A Spiritual Geography.* Boston: Houghton Mifflin Company, 1993.

"Online Finger Meditation Tool," Veriditas at Grace Cathedral, http://www.gracecathedral.org/labyrinth/interactions/index.shtml.

Papert, Seymour. *The Children's Machine: Rethinking School In the Age of the Computer.* New York: Harper Collins, 1995.

Parks, Sharon Daloz. *Big Questions, Worthy Dreams: Mentoring Young Adults in Their Search for Meaning, Purpose, and Faith.* San Francisco: Jossey-Bass, 2000.

Patte, Daniel, ed. *Global Bible Commentary.* Nashville: Abingdon, 2004.

Pavlov, Ivan P. "Conditioned Reflexes: An Investigation of the Physiological Activity of the Cerebral Cortex: Lecture XXIII," *Classics in the History of Psychology,* http://psychclassics.yorku.ca/Pavlov/lecture23.htm.

"People and Discoveries: Ivan Pavlov," A Science Odyssey, PBS Web site, http://www.pbs.org/wgbh/aso/databank/entries/bhpavl.html.

"People and Discoveries: John Watson," A Science Odyssey, PBS Web site, http://www.pbs.org/wgbh/aso/databank/entries/bhwats.html.

Perry, William. *Forms of Intellectual and Ethical Development in the College Years: A Scheme.* San Francisco: Jossey-Bass, 1999.

Piaget, Jean. *The Equilibration of Cognitive Structures.* Chicago: University of Chicago Press, 1985.

Pinar, William F. *What is Curriculum Theory?* Mahwah, NJ: Lawrence Erlbaum Associates, 2004.

Pinar, William F., and Madeleine Grumet. *Toward a Poor Curriculum.* Dubuque, Iowa: Kendell/Hunt, 1976.

Prigogine, Ilya. *Order out of Chaos: Man's New Dialogue with Nature.* Boston: Shambhala, 1984.

Quinn, Robert E. *Deep Change: Discovering the Leader Within.* San Francisco: Jossey-Bass, 1996.

Reynolds, Craig. "Boids: Background and Update," http://www.red3d.com/cwr/boids/.

Rheingold, Howard. *Tools for Thought.* Boston: MIT Press, 2000.

———. *Tools for Thought.* "Chapter Five Ex-Prodigies and Antiaircraft Guns," http://www.rheingold.com/texts/tft/5.html.

Riever, R. W. *The Individual, Communication, and Society: Essays in Memory of Gregory Bateson.* New York: Cambridge University Press, 1989.

Saward, Jeff. *Ancient Labyrinths of the World.* Thundersley, England: Caerdroia, 1997.

————. *Magical Paths: Labyrinths and Mazes in the 21st Century*. London: Mitchell Beazley, 2002.

Saward, Jeff, and Kimberly Saward. "Labyrinthos," the Labyrinth Resource Centre, http://www.labyrinthos.net.

Schultz, Duane. *A History of Modern Psychology*. 2nd ed. New York: Academic Press, 1975.

Schultz, Duane P., and Sydney Ellen Schultz. *A History of Modern Psychology (with Info Trac)*. 8th ed. New York: Wadsworth Publishing, 2003.

Schwartz, Peter, and James Ogilvy. *The Emergent Paradigm: Changing Patterns of Thought and Belief*. VALS Report No. 7. Menlo Park, CA: Values and Lifestyles Program, 1979.

Segovia, Fernando F., ed. *They Were All Together in One Place? Toward Minority Biblical Criticism*. Semeia Studies. Atlanta: Society of Biblical Literature, 2008.

Siegel, Daniel J. *The Developing Mind: How Relationships and the Brain Interact to Shape Who We Are*. New York: Guilford Press, 2001.

Simon, Uriel. *Jonah, The JPS Bible Commentary*. Philadelphia: Jewish Publication Society, 1999.

Simonaitis, Susan M. "Teaching as Conversation," in *The Scope of Our Art: The Vocation of the Theological Teacher*. Grand Rapids, MI: Wm. B. Eerdmans Publishing Co., 2002.

Skinner, B.F. "A Brief Survey of Operant Behavior," B.F. Skinner Foundation, http://www.bfskinner.org/brief_survey.html.

Slattery, Patrick. *Curriculum Development in the Postmodern Era*. 2nd ed. New York: Routledge, 2006.

Stuart, Douglas K. "Exegesis." *The Anchor Bible Dictionary*, edited by David Noel Freedman. New York: Doubleday, 1992.

————. *Old Testament Exegesis: A Handbook for Students and Pastors*. 1st ed. 1980 and 2nd ed. 1984. Louisville: Westminster John Knox Press, 2001.

Taylor, Barbara Brown. *The Luminous Web: Essays on Science and Religion*. Boston: Cowley Publications, 2000.

"Tenana River," The Doty family Web site, http://www.doty.org/travel/alaska99/tenana%20river.jpg.

Toffler, Alvin. *Future Shock*. New York: Random House, 1970.

van Manen, Max. *The Tact of Teaching: The Meaning of Pedagogical*

Thoughtfulness. Ontario: University of Western Ontario Press, 1991.

Vargas, Julie S. "A Brief Biography of B.F. Skinner," B.F. Skinner Foundation, http://www.bfskinner.org/brief_biography.html.

Voolich, Johanna, and Robert L. Devaney. "The Chaos Game," Boston University Department of Mathematics and Statistics, http://math.bu.edu/DYSYS/applets/chaos-game.html.

Vygotsky, Lev. *Mind in Society: The Development of Higher Psychological Processes.* Cambridge: Harvard University Press, 1978.

"Watson's Childhood," Furman University Psychology Department, http://alpha.furman.edu/~einstein/watson/watson2.htm.

Watzlowick, Paul, John Weakland, and Richard Fisch. *Change: Principles of Problem Formation and Problem Resolution.* New York: W. W. Norton, 1988.

West, Gerald O., ed. *Reading Other-Wise: Socially Engaged Biblical Scholars Reading with Their Local Communities.* Atlanta: Society of Biblical Literature, 2007.

Whyte, L. L. *The Unconscious Before Freud.* London: Julian Friedmann Publishers, 1960.

Wiener, Norbert. *Cybernetics: or, The Control and Communication in the Animal and the Machine.* 2nd ed. Boston: MIT Press, 1965.

Williams, Andrew. "Computing the Mandelbrot Set," *Plus Magazine,* September 1999. Mandelbrot series: http://plus.maths.org/issue9/features/mandelbrot/.

Wilson, Edward O., ed. *From So Simple a Beginning: Darwin's Four Great Books.* New York: W. W. Norton, 2005.

Winston, Patrick Henry, and Berthold Klaus Horn., *LISP.* 2nd ed. Reading, MA: Addison Wesley, 1984.

Wozniak, Robert H. "Mind and Body: Rene Déscartes to William James," Serendip, http://serendip.brynmawr.edu/Mind/. Originally published in 1992 at Bethesda, MD and Washington, DC by the National Library of Medicine and the American Psychological Association.

Yee, Gale A., ed. *Judges & Method: New Approaches in Biblical Studies.* 2nd ed. Minneapolis: Fortress Press, 2007.

Index

Italicized page numbers indicate illustrations. Endnotes are indicated with "n" followed by the endnote number.

About the Authors

Sherrie Reynolds is a Professor of Educational Psychology at Texas Christian University. Her research interests include learning, change, the new science, and social justice issues, including gender. She has numerous publications, including the book *Learning is a Verb: The Psychology of Teaching and Learning* and the chapter "Patterns that Connect: A Recursive Epistemology" in William C. Doll Jr., M. Jayne Fleener, Donna Trueit, and John St. Julien's book *Chaos, Complexity, Curriculum, and Culture.*

Toni Craven is the I. Wiley and Elizabeth M. Briscoe Chair and Professor of Hebrew Bible at Brite Divinity School, Texas Christian University. She is a member of the Catholic Biblical Association and the Society of Biblical Literature. Her research interests include gender issues and rhetorical/literary study, as well as teaching and learning. She has numerous publications and served as an associate editor of *Women in Scripture: A Dictionary of Named and Unnamed Women in the Hebrew Bible, the Apocryphal/Deuterocanonical Books, and the New Testament.*

Credits

ISBN 978-0-87565-391-4

Higher Education Reconceived
ISBN 978-0-87565-391-4
Paper. $16.95.